Python

For Key Stage Three

Speaking to snakes isn't easy. Trust us, we've tried. But when it comes to programming languages, this CGP book will help you be fluent in no time...

We've made the perfect step-by-step guide to coding in Python — it's full of examples, practice questions and coding challenges, with full answers at the back.

And if that wasn't enough, we've also included a digital goody bag packed with downloadable Python files, helpful videos for the trickiest problems and a free Online Edition of the whole book! No, you're not dreaming — it's all `True`.

Unlock your Digital Extras

Just scan a QR code in the book to get your digital extras. Or go to cgpbooks.co.uk/extras and enter this code to unlock your Online Edition!

0378 8626 5844 5355

By the way, this code only works for one person. If somebody else has used this book before you, they might have already claimed the code.

Programming Guide

Contents

Section One — Introducing Python
What is Python?...2
Installing Python...3
The Shell Window..4
The Editor Window..5
Common Errors..6
Your First Program...7
Algorithms..8
Practice Questions..9

Section Two — Outputs, Inputs and Variables
Printing on Screen...10
Collecting User Input...11
Practice Questions..12
What is a Variable?..13
Using Variables...14
Practice Questions..15
Controlling On-Screen Text.................................16
Practice Questions..17
Coding Challenges for Section Two.....................18

Section Three — Data Types and Operators
Data Types..19
How to Handle Strings......................................20
Practice Questions..22
Working with Integers and Floats........................23
Practice Questions..25
Relational Operators...26
Boolean Operators..27
Practice Questions..28
Coding Challenges for Section Three...................29

Section Four — Selection
Selection...30
if Statements...31
Practice Questions..32
The else Clause..33
The elif Clause...34
Practice Questions..35
Coding Challenges for Section Four....................36

Section Five — Iteration
Iteration..37
for Loops..38
Practice Questions..39
Printing Numbers and Letters..............................40
Practice Questions..42
Coding Challenges for Section Five.....................43

Section Six — More Iteration
More Iteration..44
while Loops...45
Nesting Statements...47
Practice Questions..48
Coding Challenges for Section Six......................49

Section Seven — Lists
Lists...50
Working with Lists..51
Practice Questions..52
Iterating through Lists.......................................53
2D Lists..54
Practice Questions..55
Coding Challenges for Section Seven..................56

Section Eight — Subroutines
Built-in Subroutines..57
Practice Questions..59
Defining Subroutines...60
Parameters..62
Return Values..63
Practice Questions..64
Coding Challenges for Section Eight...................65

Contents

Section Nine — Turtle Graphics
Basic Commands 66
Simple Shapes 67
Practice Questions 69
Polygons and Circles 70
Adding Colours 71
Stars and Random Shapes 72
Practice Questions 73
Coding Challenges for Section Nine 74

Section Ten — Longer Challenges
Worked Challenges 75
Independent Challenges 77

Python Quick Reference Guide 81
Glossary 82
Answers 83
Index 93

There are lots of **additional files** for use with this book. These include the example Python programs that you'll see on the pages, Python programs that are example answers for questions or challenges and a few .txt files too.

You can find the **full set of these files** at cgpbooks.co.uk/ks3-python-extras

You can also access all of the files by scanning this **QR code**.

Published by CGP

Based on the classic CGP style created by Richard Parsons.

Written by Alex Brown and Paul Clowrey.

Editors: Michael Bushell, Sammy El-Bahrawy, Andy Hurst and Chris Lindle.
Reviewer: Tim Dudley.
With thanks to Shaun Harrogate, Pam Jones and Simon Little for the proofreading.
With thanks to Alice Dent for the copyright research.

Python screenshots used with permission of the PSF.
Linux® is the registered trademark of Linus Torvalds in the U.S. and other countries.
macOS is a trademark of Apple Inc., registered in the U.S. and other countries.
Microsoft® and Windows® are trademarks of the Microsoft group of companies.
Mozilla is a trademark of the Mozilla Foundation in the US and other countries.

ISBN: 978 1 83774 065 9

Printed by Elanders Ltd, Newcastle upon Tyne.
Clipart from Corel®

Text, design, layout and original illustrations © Coordination Group Publications Ltd (CGP) 2023
All rights reserved.

Photocopying more than one section of this book is not permitted, even if you have a CLA licence.
Extra copies are available from CGP with next day delivery • 0800 1712 712 • www.cgpbooks.co.uk

Section One — Introducing Python

What is Python?

Learning Objectives

Before you start writing programs, let's take a look at what Python is, where it came from, and why it's a fantastic programming language to learn.
- Learn about the history of Python.
- Understand the purpose of Python.
- Learn about where Python is used today.
- Understand why it is worth learning Python.

Python has been developed for over 30 years

1) Python was first released in 1991 by Guido van Rossum.
2) It's an open-source language, meaning it's free to use and adapt.
3) Version 3 is the latest and it gets small updates every few months.
4) It has become a popular programming language that's taught in schools around the world.

Python is a textual programming language

1) Textual programming languages are ones that use words as commands, unlike some other visual programming languages you might have used (like Scratch™).
2) It was designed to use commands that people easily understand — e.g. `print`, `input` and `if` — so that it could be used by people of all abilities to write programs of all sizes.
3) It can be used to create all sorts of programs, such as games, web apps and artificial intelligence systems like chatbots.

Python is popular around the world

1) Many teachers are using Python as their language of choice.
2) Python is used by real programmers in a range of industries, including science, medicine and finance.
3) You might have heard of these world-wide users of Python: Google, Facebook, Instagram, Netflix™, Spotify® and NASA.

Q1 Search for three other companies that use Python as part of the programs they make.

Learning Python has many benefits

- Python builds on top of the skills you may already have from using visual programming languages.
- It teaches you logical thinking skills and problem solving.
- It can be used in GCSE Computer Science courses.
- It is completely free and open source.
- There is an enormous online community, offering support and tutorials.

KEY TERMS — Open source software is free to download, share and edit in any way.

And there you were thinking you'd be wrangling snakes...

You don't need an expensive computer and a University degree to be a real programmer. Python makes programming easy and accessible to everyone, and it's absolutely free.

Installing Python

Learning Objectives

Python is free to use and widely available. Follow this guide to get yourself set up and you'll be all ready to program like... erm... like a programmer.

- Learn how to download and install Python.
- Learn about IDLE — the software used in this book.
- Learn about the other ways you can use Python.

How to install Python

1) Python should be downloaded from the Python website — the latest version can be found at: www.python.org/downloads/
2) There are versions available for most operating systems, such as Windows®, macOS and Linux®.
3) Run the installer after it has downloaded and follow the on-screen instructions.

Python is FREE. Be wary of any website asking for money to download it.

IDLE comes free with Python

- When you install Python, you also get the option to install a program called IDLE.
- IDLE is an Integrated Development Environment (IDE) — that sounds fancy, but it's actually quite a simple bit of software designed for beginners.
- It has two key parts: the Editor window (for typing code) and the Shell window (for running code).

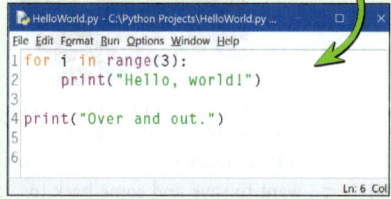 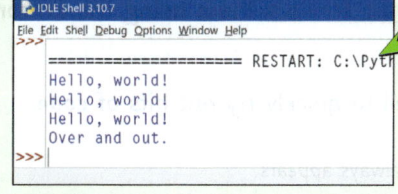

See pages 4 and 5 for more about these.

- The code in this book was written and tested using IDLE, but many other Python IDEs exist (both free and paid for) and could be used instead.

Scan to watch our video guide on using IDLE.

Python can be installed on many devices

1) Python programmers typically use an IDE on a desktop or laptop computer.
2) But it doesn't stop there — Python can also be used on:
    - Mini-computers like the Raspberry Pi.
    - Websites that allow you to type and test code in a web browser.
    - Smartphone apps that include tutorials and testing windows.
    - Graphing calculators — some come with Python preinstalled.

Popular browser-based Python IDEs include Replit, Programiz, trinket and W3Schools.

I installed Python on my bionic leg — it runs just fine...

There's lots of Python code floating about online and it's not all safe to use. Don't just copy and run any old code you find — always check where it came from, and read and understand it first.

Section One — Introducing Python

The Shell Window

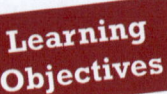

Hopefully you've managed to install Python by now, because if haven't you'll be playing on hard mode for the rest of this book. This page is all about the Shell.
- Understand the purpose of the Shell.
- Understand how the Shell links to the Editor.
- Learn about how to use the Shell to test simple code.

The Shell shows the output of programs...

1) The IDLE Shell is a preview window that runs within IDLE.
2) You type your program into the Editor (see the next page) and the Shell shows what happens when the program is run.
3) This means if there is a problem with your program, your computer won't crash — the program just stops running within IDLE.
4) You'll see lots of example programs in this book. The Editor and Shell will be shown together like this.

In this book we will refer to the Shell window as the 'Shell' and the Editor window as the 'Editor'.

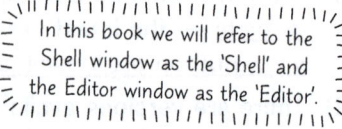

...and it deals with input too

Input is data entered into a computer.
Output is data given back by a computer.

It's not all about output — the Shell is used for input too:
1) If your program requires user input when running, e.g. getting the answer to a question, the user will type into the Shell when asked.
2) You can also type code directly into the Shell. This means you can test lines of code without having to save them using the Editor.

EXAMPLE Using the Shell to quickly try out bits of code.

You should use the Editor for writing longer programs that you want to save and come back to.

Computer system information always appears at the top of the Shell — you can ignore it.

```
Python 3.10.7 (tags/v3.10.7:6cc6b13, Sep  5 2022, 14:08:36) [MSC v.1933 64 bit (AMD64)] on win32
Type "help", "copyright", "credits" or "license()" for more information.
>>> print("This is the Shell.")
This is the Shell.
>>>
```

A line of code is typed straight into the Shell where the characters >>> appear.

Any output is displayed directly underneath the code, after pressing the Return key.

The output of these bits of code is explained on p.16 and p.23.

Q1 Use the Shell to find the output of the following code.

a) `>>> print("3" + "5")`   b) `>>> print(223 * 307)`

Input and output — that's Python in a nutshell...

If you see >>> then you're in the Shell, not the Editor. The Shell is a handy tool for testing bits of code without having to save a file, but you should use the Editor for anything you want to keep.

Section One — Introducing Python

The Editor Window

> **Learning Objectives**
>
> The Editor is where the magic happens — or will happen, eventually, once you've worked through this book. Your sorcery may be a bit scruffy for a while yet.
> - Understand the purpose of the Editor and how it links to the Shell.
> - Learn how to create, save, run and edit programs in the Editor.
> - Learn about the features the Editor has to help you program.

Write and run programs from the Editor

1) The IDLE Editor is where you write, edit and save your code.
2) It will give you tips and formatting advice to help you write programs.

How to program in four easy steps

When you start IDLE, you'll usually see the Shell window. The process to open the Editor and create a new program is always the same.

EXAMPLE How to use the IDLE Editor to make and run programs.

From the Shell window, go to the File menu and click 'New File'. The Editor will open with an empty window.

Type your code in the Editor window. The program on p.7 is a great one to try first.

You'll need to save your program before IDLE will even think about running it. Click 'Save As' from the File menu and choose a sensible name.

Python programs are saved with the .py file extension.

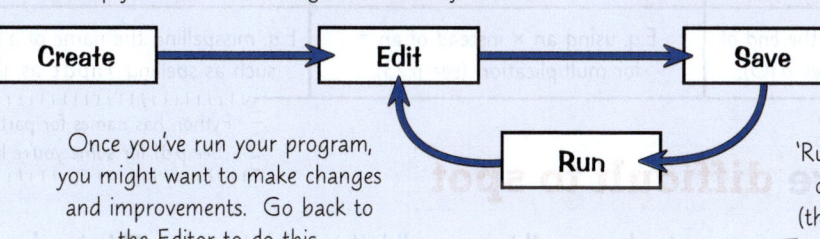

Once you've run your program, you might want to make changes and improvements. Go back to the Editor to do this.

Run your program by clicking 'Run Module' from the Run menu, or using the keyboard shortcut (the one shown in the Run menu). The Shell will pop up with the results.

Eric didn't follow the four easy steps...

The Editor has lots of useful features

- **Auto-indentation** — sometimes Python code needs to be formatted in a particular way, with lines requiring space at the beginning (see p.31). The Editor will take care of this for you.
- **Code completion tips** — if the Editor recognises code you're typing, options for completing it will appear as you type.
- **Visual customisation** — you can change the way the Editor looks, including background colours, font styles and whether to show or hide line numbers (p.7). 'Dark mode' is a favourite of night owls.
- **Syntax highlighting** — colouring different bits of code, making it easier to read and easier to spot errors.
- **Error checking** — when you run your program, it will automatically be checked for certain syntax errors (see the next page). The Editor will stop the program from running and display the first syntax error it finds.

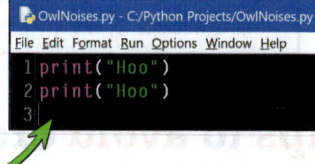

Don't worry about understanding all of these features yet, they will be explained as you work through the book.

Eat, sleep, and breathe Python — or just casually enjoy it...

Many programmers place the Editor and Shell windows besides each other on the screen when using IDLE. That way you can easily see everything at once — it's an efficient way to program.

Common Errors

Learning Objectives

I'm not going to lie, a lot can (and usually does) go wrong when programming, especially when starting out. Learning to spot and prevent errors will make everything smoother.
- Learn what a program error is.
- Understand the difference between syntax errors and logic errors.
- Learn ways to avoid making errors when programming.

Program errors are part of programming

1) A program error is anything that will cause a program to stop, crash, or behave unexpectedly because it has broken the rules or has done something you didn't mean for it to do.
2) There are two main types of program error: syntax errors and logic errors.

Breaking the rules causes a syntax error

1) Python, like all programming languages, has a set of rules and commands that it understands.
2) If you type something that Python doesn't recognise, this breaks the rules and causes a syntax error.
3) IDLE will spot syntax errors and they will prevent a program from being run.
4) Some of the common syntax errors include:

Missing an important character	Using an incorrect character	Making a simple typing mistake
E.g. missing the bracket at the end of a `print()` statement (see p.10).	E.g. using an × instead of an * for multiplication (see p.23)	E.g. misspelling the name of a function, such as spelling `input` as `imput`.

Python has names for particular errors. See p.81 for some you're likely to see.

Logic errors are difficult to spot

1) A logic error causes your program to do something you didn't intend it to do. This is when your instructions make sense to Python, but you aren't asking it to do what you really want it to.
2) Logic errors won't prevent your programming from being run — IDLE will assume everything is fine.
3) Examples of common logic errors are:

Using the wrong values	Using incorrect calculations	Getting stuck in a cycle
E.g. setting the number of days in a week to 6, rather than 7.	E.g. doing addition where you should have done subtraction.	E.g. the condition to exit a loop is never met, so it keeps repeating forever.

Tips to avoid creating errors in your programs

- Check spelling and punctuation — e.g. the built-in Python functions are all lowercase.
- Check variable names (p.13) — make sure they match exactly if they're repeated in a program.
- Check index values (p.21) — it's really easy to be off-by-one with these.
- Check indentation (p.31) — particularly any lines following colons.

Any errors on this page were left for you to spot — honesst...

Create an error spotting checklist to check your own code. As you get more experience, you'll figure out which mistakes you make the most often — highlight these for a double check.

Your First Program

Learning Objectives

Enough stalling... It's time to get you programming in Python. Don't worry about understanding every detail right away — it will all be explained later in the book.
- Be able to use the Editor to create and run a simple program.
- Learn about line numbers and why they're useful.
- Learn how errors are presented in this book and in the Shell.

Your first Python program

1) Since the 1970s, the 'Hello, world!' program has been the first for many new programmers.
2) Simply type this code into the Editor, save, then run it to view the result in the Shell.

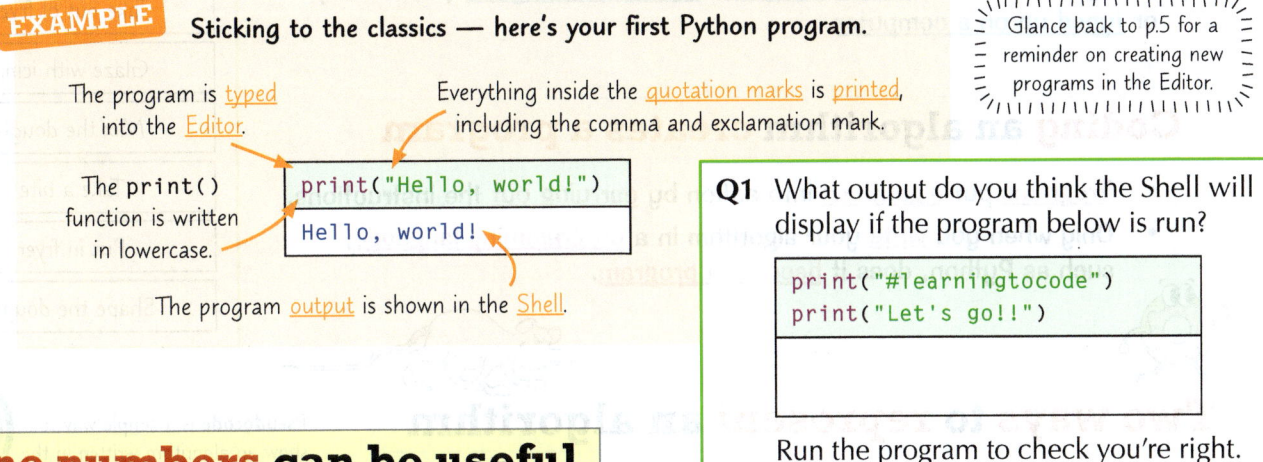

EXAMPLE Sticking to the classics — here's your first Python program.

The program is typed into the Editor.

The print() function is written in lowercase.

```
print("Hello, world!")
```
```
Hello, world!
```

Everything inside the quotation marks is printed, including the comma and exclamation mark.

The program output is shown in the Shell.

Glance back to p.5 for a reminder on creating new programs in the Editor.

Q1 What output do you think the Shell will display if the program below is run?

```
print("#learningtocode")
print("Let's go!!")
```

Run the program to check you're right.

Line numbers can be useful

- Some programs in this book show line numbers.
```
1  print("Line 1!")
2  print("Line 2!")
```
- They're not part of the code, so shouldn't be copied, but they're useful for talking about it.
- You can turn on line numbers in the Editor from the 'Options' menu.

A note about errors

```
print)"ERROR!("
```
```
SyntaxError: unmatched ')'
```

1) This book has some examples with intentional errors.
2) The Editor and Shell for these will be shown with a red border.
3) In IDLE, errors will either pop up in the Editor, or be output in the Shell.

Q2 Each of the programs below contains an error.

```
PRINT("Bonjour le monde")
```
```
print("Hola Mundo"]
```
```
prinnt("Konnichiwa sekai")
```

Circle and describe the errors, then run each program in the Shell to see how the error is shown and what IDLE has to say.

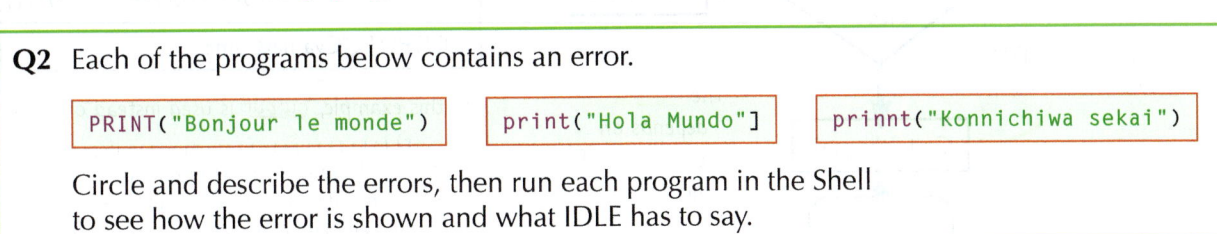

1 print("Dear Diary, today I became a Python programmer...")

Line numbers can be useful when you're talking to others about your programs, or when trying to track down a pesky bug in your code. Many error messages in IDLE will include the line number.

Section One — Introducing Python

Algorithms

Learning Objectives

Jumping straight into IDLE and typing up a storm is a recipe for a poor program. Good programmers plan ahead and think through their algorithms first.

- Understand what an algorithm is.
- Learn the difference between an algorithm and a program.
- Be able to represent an algorithm as a flowchart.
- Be able to represent an algorithm in pseudocode.

An algorithm is a series of instructions

1) Algorithms are sets of clear instructions that solve problems.
2) An algorithm can be written on paper, drawn as a diagram (see below) or typed up on a computer.

Coding an algorithm creates a program

- Programs put algorithms into action by carrying out the instructions.
- Only when you write your algorithm in a programming language, such as Python, does it become a program.

Q1 Put these steps in order to show how to make doughnuts.

| Take out of fryer |
| Glaze with icing |
| Mix the dough |
| Take a bite |
| Put in fryer |
| Shape the dough |

Two ways to represent an algorithm

Here are two ways to plan out an algorithm before writing a program.

KEY TERMS: Pseudocode is a simple way to show an algorithm written in the style of a programming language.

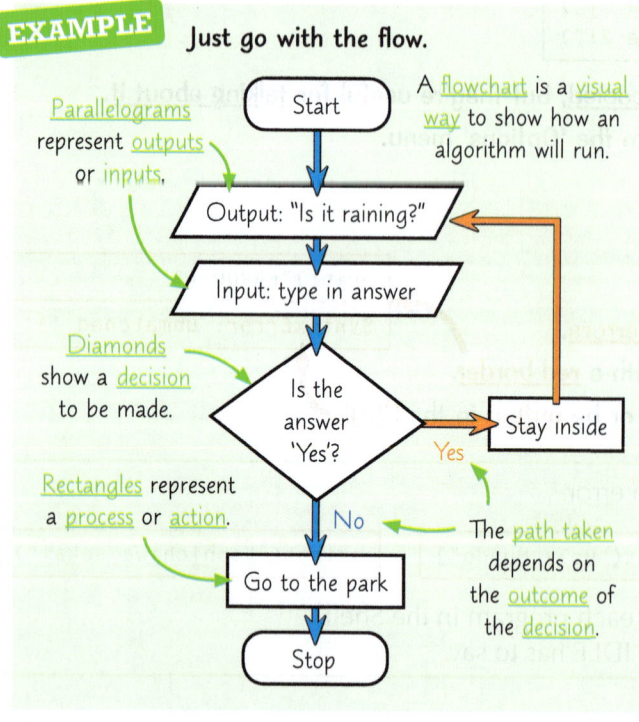

EXAMPLE Just go with the flow.

A flowchart is a visual way to show how an algorithm will run.

Parallelograms represent outputs or inputs.

Diamonds show a decision to be made.

Rectangles represent a process or action.

The path taken depends on the outcome of the decision.

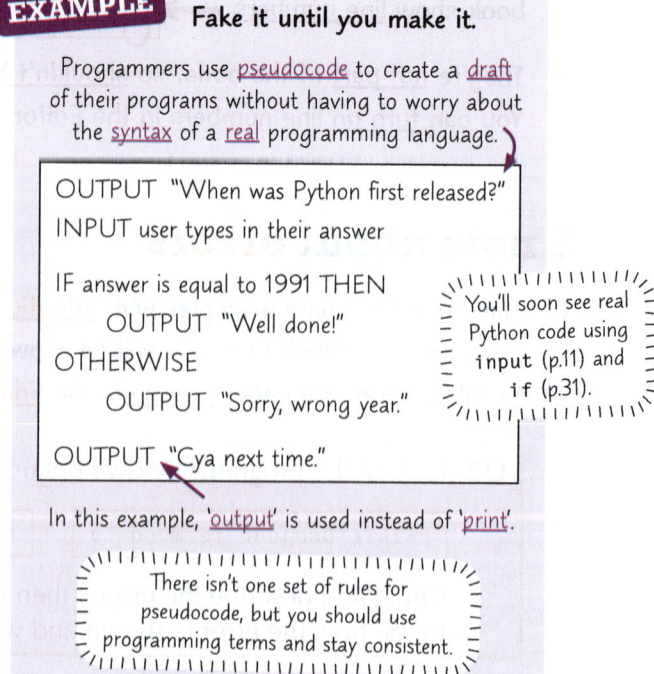

EXAMPLE Fake it until you make it.

Programmers use pseudocode to create a draft of their programs without having to worry about the syntax of a real programming language.

```
OUTPUT "When was Python first released?"
INPUT user types in their answer

IF answer is equal to 1991 THEN
    OUTPUT "Well done!"
OTHERWISE
    OUTPUT "Sorry, wrong year."

OUTPUT "Cya next time."
```

You'll soon see real Python code using input (p.11) and if (p.31).

In this example, 'output' is used instead of 'print'.

There isn't one set of rules for pseudocode, but you should use programming terms and stay consistent.

I hope you got Q1 sorted or you'll end up with pseudoughnuts...

Programmers dream of writing shiny new code — not sorting out errors in buggy old stuff. The better you plan algorithms, the better your programs will be, so get out there and live the dream.

Practice Questions

Warm-Up

Q1 True or false? Python and IDLE are free and open source.

Q2 What is the file extension for Python code files?

Q3 What is an error that breaks the rules of a program language called?

Q4 What does a parallelogram in a flowchart represent: input and output, a decision, or a process?

Practice Questions

Q1 List three devices that can be used to write and run Python.

1. ....
2. ....
3. ....

Q2 Explain why you would use the Editor instead of the Shell when writing longer programs.

....

....

Q3 Name three features of the Editor that can help you when writing code.

1. ....
2. ....
3. ....

Q4 Which of these bits of Python code contains a syntax error? Write 'Yes' or 'No' for each.

Python Code	Syntax Error?
`print("Paris is the UK capital.")`	
`print(^Hello, world!^)`	
`PRINT("What is your age?")`	
`print("I am -13 years old.")`	

Don't worry if you don't fully understand all the code yet, just compare with the program on p.7 to decide on your answer.

Q5 An algorithm is a sequence of step-by-step instructions

a) What is the key difference between an algorithm and a program?

....

....

b) Give one reason for using pseudocode rather than actual code.

....

....

Section One — Introducing Python

Section Two — Outputs, Inputs and Variables

Printing on Screen

Learning Objectives

Let's start with getting the basics down — showing a message on screen. We'll then talk about a few ways you might mess that up, and how you can spot when you do.
- Be able to use the print function to output text on screen.
- Understand the use of colour in IDLE for Python code.

Use print() to show text on screen

1) You've already seen print used in your first program on page 7.
2) It tells the computer to display any message placed in the quotation marks.

EXAMPLE Getting the structure right from the start is key to programming.

The quotation marks tell the computer where the message begins and ends.

```
print("EVERYTHING in the quotes is shown on screen.")
EVERYTHING in the quotes is shown on screen.
```

Double quotes are used in this book, but you can use single quotes too — they work just the same.

3) You could write this in the Shell without saving, but as you start to make longer programs, it makes more sense to write your code in the Editor so you can save it — see page 5 for a reminder of this process.

Q1 Write the line of code that will create the message shown.

```
One function in the bag!
```

Use colouring to help spot mistakes

1) You may have noticed that IDLE displays Python code in colour.
2) This isn't part of Python itself — it's a feature of IDLE that helps you identify different elements in your code.
3) You don't need to learn the colours but they're great for spotting errors.

```
print("Hello there")
print(Hello there")
```

The top line is correct while the line below isn't, so the colours are different.

COMMON PROBLEMS

Here are a couple of ways that printing can go terribly wrong.

```
print("Hello there')
SyntaxError: unterminated string
literal (detected at line 1)
```

You can use single or double quotes, but not both.

Always check your function spelling.

```
prmt("Hello there")
NameError: name 'prmt' is not
defined. Did you mean: 'print'?
```

IDLE will offer solutions to some errors.

Q2 Which of the following lines is correct?
1. Print("Is it me?")
2. print("Is it me?)
3. print("Is it me?")
4. print"(Is it me?)"

You will see print() used on p.13 without quote marks when using variables.

Too much outputting can be off-putting in polite company...
This book sticks to the default colour scheme in IDLE, but it doesn't matter which colours you use. They can be changed in the IDLE preferences if you fancy a different look — you do you.

Collecting User Input

Learning Objectives
The `print` function is used for showing information, so it would make sense for there to be a function for getting information too — and whaddaya know, there is.
- Understand the purpose of the `input` function.
- Be able to combine inputting and outputting in one program.
- Be able to describe uses for the `input` function.

input() allows users to respond to questions

1) Many programs work in the same way: something is input, the computer does something with it, and an output is created.
2) Use the `input` function when you want the user to type something into your program.

EXAMPLE `input` is structured in the same way as `print`.

Both functions use brackets and quotation marks.

The message within the quotes is displayed on screen and the computer will then wait for a response.

```
input("What is your name?")
What is your name?
```

Combine input and output to create a conversation

1) Unlike a `print` message that's just meant to be read, an `input` message requires a response.
2) Combining `input` and `print` functions lets you create your first interactive program.

EXAMPLE This sequence of printing and user input creates a basic chatbot.

The first line is simply displayed on screen.

The next line requires input, so the program will stop until a response is typed and the Return key is pressed.

```
print("Hello, my name is CGPbot.")
input("What is your name?")
print("Wow! Hope to chat again soon.")

Hello, my name is CGPbot.
What is your name?Grace
Wow! Hope to chat again soon.
```

The program stops and waits for the user to type in their name.

KEY TERMS
A **chatbot** is a program designed to mimic conversation with users online.

Q1 Create your own chatbot that asks the user two questions.

Use input to add interactivity to programs

You will see the `input` function used a lot throughout this book. Examples of where it could be used include:
- Question and answer programs, like the chatbot above.
- As part of mathematical calculations, e.g. in a calculator program (p.24).
- Building lists of data (see Section 7), such as a contacts list.
- Drawing using turtle graphics (you'll make these later in Section 9).

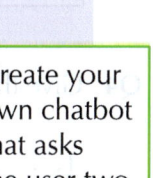
Who am I? What am I?

Hey, CGPbot — input that pizza straight into my mouth...

The `print` and `input` functions will get you writing your first real programs. These pages covered the basics of using them, but keep reading — you'll soon discover they can do a whole lot more.

Section Two — Outputs, Inputs and Variables

Practice Questions

Warm-Up

Q1 Will this line of code run correctly? `print(Hello there")`

Q2 Will typing `print` incorrectly as `pri nt` create a logic or a syntax error?

Q3 How does IDLE make different bits of code look different?

Q4 What is a program designed to recreate human conversation often called?

Q5 Which key on the keyboard needs to be pressed after typing a response to an `input` question?

Practice Questions

Q1 What does the `print` function do?

....

....

Q2 Tick whether the following statements are True or False.

Statement	True	False
Single quote marks can't be used with the `print` function.		
Colours in IDLE can be used to help spot syntax errors.		
This line of code contains an error: `print('Yo!")`		

See p.6 for a reminder on the different types of errors in programming.

Q3 Fill in the blanks to complete the program below.

```
input.........What is your favourite colour? ")
.................................Thank you, I won't remember that..........
What is your favourite colour? Startled-salmon pink
Thank you, I won't remember that.
```

Q4 Give three types of programs that might use the `input` function.

1. ....

2. ....

3. ....

Q5 An idea for a chatbot program has been written below.
Write a program that will carry out all the instructions.

Chatbot says "I'm going to ask some questions."

Chatbot asks "What is your name?"

Chatbot responds "Cool name..."

Chatbot asks "Do you put pineapple on pizza?"

Chatbot response "I'm the same!"

Section Two — Outputs, Inputs and Variables

What is a Variable?

Learning Objectives

How many times are you going to have to type your name? Can't a program just remember it? Yes, it certainly can, but first you'll need to learn about variables.

- Understand what a variable is and what it can contain.
- Learn how to name a variable and to follow naming conventions.
- Be able to change the value of a variable.

Conventions are rules that most people have agreed to follow.

KEY TERMS

Every variable needs a name and a value

1) A variable is a name within a program that contains a value.
2) You can use them to store all sorts of things, like numbers, letters and words.
3) Imagine them as a box with a label (the name) and a value inside.

EXAMPLE Assigning values to variables and displaying them.

The name of the variable goes before the equals sign.

Printing the value of a variable doesn't need quotation marks, just the name.

```
animal = "Camel"
humps = 2
print(animal)
print(humps)

Camel
2
```

The value you're assigning goes after the equals sign.

Numbers don't need quotation marks. See p.19 for more about data types.

Follow these rules when naming variables

- Variable names should have no spaces and cannot start with a number.
- The only symbol you can use is the underscore (_).
- Capital letters make a difference — e.g. word and Word aren't the same variable.
- Decide on a naming convention and stick with it in your program.

EXAMPLE Most programmers use one of three naming conventions:

Upper camel case capitalises the first letter of every word.

```
FirstName = "Eli"
```

Lower camel case capitalises the first letters of the second word onwards.

```
firstName = "Eli"
```

Snake case uses an underscore between words.

```
first_name = "Eli"
```

Q1 Which of these are valid variable names?

first name	1stNAME
surname	Surname?
name1	#name

Variable values can be changed

1) The value assigned to a variable is not fixed. It can be changed in the same program.
2) If a variable appears more than once in a program, its name must match exactly each time it is used.

EXAMPLE Imagine you've aged 5 years in a second.

The value of age is changed from 11 to 16.

Each time the variable is printed it displays the current value.

```
age = 11
print(age)
age = 16
print(age)

11
16
```

My parents are programmers — they named me "Child3"...

Follow the rules and stick to a naming convention and you'll be mostly sorted, but it's also worth giving your variables readable names. Code like `brkfst = "pancakes"` isn't easy to understand.

Section Two — Outputs, Inputs and Variables

Using Variables

Learning Objectives

Your programs are about to step up a gear. As teased on the previous page, you now know enough to ask a question and have your program remember the answer.

- Be able to use variables with the `input` function and in simple calculations.
- Learn how to avoid some common errors when using variables.

Variables can hold user input...

The chatbot program on page 11 responded in a very general way. You can make it more realistic by including the user input in the response.

EXAMPLE An improved chatbot that doesn't ignore the user.

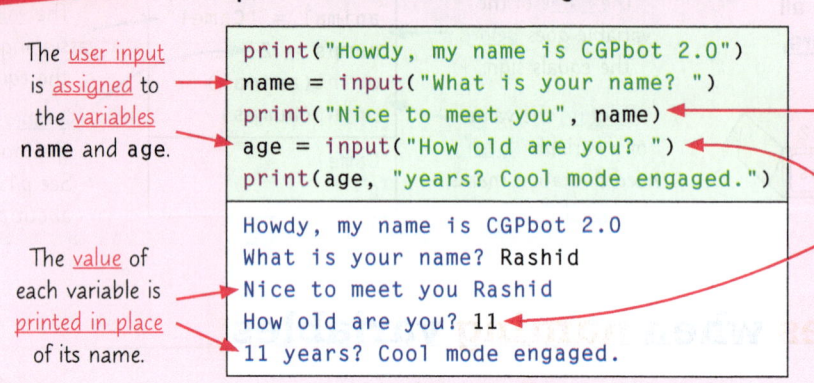

The user input is assigned to the variables name and age.

```
print("Howdy, my name is CGPbot 2.0")
name = input("What is your name? ")
print("Nice to meet you", name)
age = input("How old are you? ")
print(age, "years? Cool mode engaged.")
```

The quotation marks close and a comma is added before the variable.

The value of each variable is printed in place of its name.

```
Howdy, my name is CGPbot 2.0
What is your name? Rashid
Nice to meet you Rashid
How old are you? 11
11 years? Cool mode engaged.
```

Putting a space at the end of each question separates the user's input from the rest of the text, which looks neater.

...they can be used in calculations too

The example above stores text in variables, but you can also store numbers and carry out calculations.

EXAMPLE A program to calculate the savings of an item that's on sale.

The first two variables are holding numbers.

The value of `saving` is calculated by subtracting the value of `salePrice` from the value of `fullPrice`.

```
fullPrice = 20
salePrice = 15
saving = fullPrice - salePrice
print("You save", saving, "pounds")
```

```
You save 5 pounds
```

There are lots more examples of calculations in Python later in this book, starting on p.23.

Avoid these variable mistakes

Imagine you've woken up in 1993 and need to program a time machine. It'll be easier if you avoid these mistakes.

The name always comes first when assigning a value to a variable.

```
1993 = year
```
(and remember, variable names can't start with a number)

```
print("The year is", year)
year = 1993
NameError: name 'year' is not defined
```

You can't refer to a variable before it has been assigned a value.

Q1 Find two errors in this program.
```
name = input("Who are you?")
print(hello, username)
```

Back in '93 we were basically chiselling code into clay tablets...

When you list things to output, e.g. `print("I", "am", "awesome")`, you automatically get a space between each of the things in the list — so you'll see `I am awesome` and not `Iamawesome`. Cool eh?

Practice Questions

Warm-Up

Q1 What character should be used to assign a value to a variable?

Q2 Why would 'top speed' not work as a variable name?

Q3 Would tyrePressure and TyrePressure refer to the same or different variables?

Q4 What character is missing in this line? `print("Good morning" name)`

Q5 What is wrong with this line of code? `70 = maxSpeed`

Practice Questions

Q1 Describe the purpose of a variable.

....

Q2 Complete these sentences about using variables.

a) The only symbol you can use in a variable name is an ....

b) .... cannot be used at the start of a variable name.

Q3 Draw a line matching the naming convention to the example of a variable using it.

Upper camel case		`battery_level`
Lower camel case		`SuperCar`
Snake case		`maxHeight`

Q4 The program below calculates and prints a shopping total.

a) Complete lines 4 and 5.

```
1   apples = 5
2   bread = 2
3   milk = 3
4   shopTotal = apples + ..................... + .....................
5   print(.........................)
```

b) What total will be displayed?

....

Q5 Tick whether the following statements are True or False.

Statement	True	False
A variable can be used before it has been assigned a value.		
tOTAlsIZe does not follow any standard naming convention.		
Numbers can be used at the end of a variable name.		

Controlling On-Screen Text

Learning Objectives

So you've written a cool program, but the output on screen doesn't look right? You know, that age-old problem. Here are a few ways to sort it out.

- Be able to join text together using concatenation.
- Be able to use escape characters to change the layout of text on the screen.

Use concatenation to join pieces of text

1) The plus (+) sign is used in Python to add numbers together, as you do in maths.
2) It can also be used to combine pieces of text — this is called concatenation.
3) It doesn't try to calculate anything, it simply joins them together.

EXAMPLE Using concatenation to join two inputs to make one output.

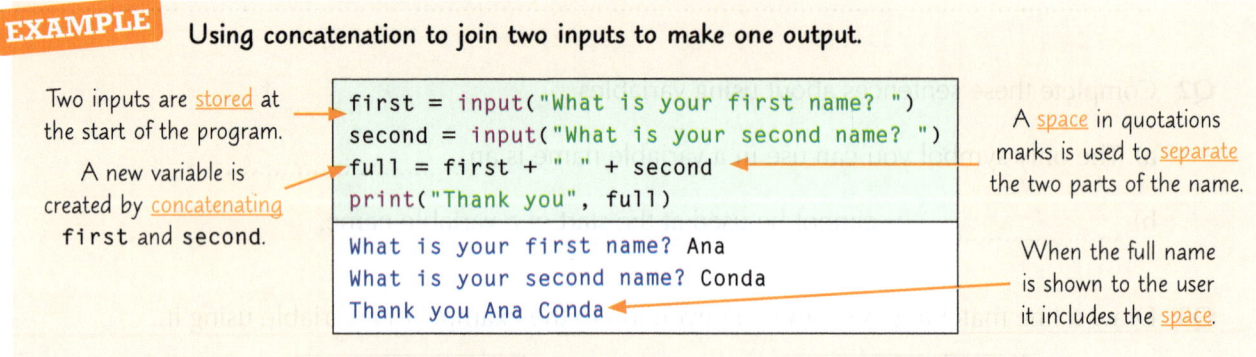

Two inputs are stored at the start of the program.

A new variable is created by concatenating `first` and `second`.

```
first = input("What is your first name? ")
second = input("What is your second name? ")
full = first + " " + second
print("Thank you", full)

What is your first name? Ana
What is your second name? Conda
Thank you Ana Conda
```

A space in quotations marks is used to separate the two parts of the name.

When the full name is shown to the user it includes the space.

Escape characters can change the way text looks

1) Printed text is displayed as a long stream of letters, numbers, symbols and spaces.
2) You cannot simply press return to add a new line when using print().
3) Instead, you need to use the escape character \n.

COMMON PROBLEMS Escape characters use a backslash (\). If you use a forward slash (/) they won't work.

EXAMPLE Here's how to use \n to your advantage.

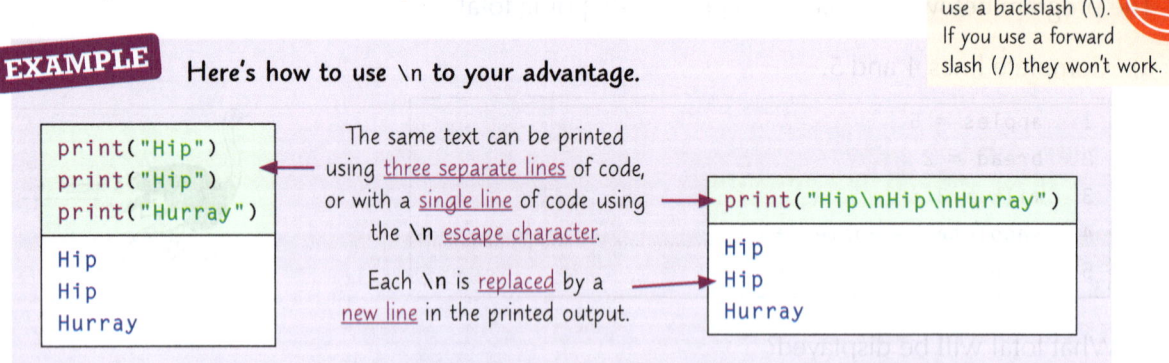

```
print("Hip")
print("Hip")
print("Hurray")
Hip
Hip
Hurray
```

The same text can be printed using three separate lines of code, or with a single line of code using the \n escape character.

Each \n is replaced by a new line in the printed output.

```
print("Hip\nHip\nHurray")
Hip
Hip
Hurray
```

GOING FURTHER Escape characters can make your programs more efficient (creating the same output but with less code). People also use them when making ASCII art (simple graphics made from letters and symbols).

Q1 Write a one-line program to make the output shown.

```
I <3
Python
```

Before \n there was Houdini — the original escape character...

You may be used to placing text and images anywhere you like when using things like word processors. Python works differently, but you can still find interesting ways to display text.

Section Two — Outputs, Inputs and Variables

Practice Questions

Warm-Up

Q1 What character is used to join two pieces of text?

Q2 What character is used when using escape characters?

Practice Questions

Q1 Describe what concatenation is and what it is used for.

....

....

Q2 This program creates a new username from the answers given.

Write down what the user would see, including the inputs that you'd write, followed by the final output.

```
partOne = input("If you mix yellow and blue you get? ")
partTwo = input("What year were you born? ")
username = partOne + partTwo
print(username)
```

Q3 You have decided to use the `\n` escape character in your new program.

a) Explain what this character does.

....

b) How can using this escape character make a program more efficient?

....

....

Q4 Circle the three errors in this program.

```
print("Choose an even number between 1 and 10 but don't tell me )
numbre = input("Type in your number and I promise not to look: ")
print("I guess your number was": number)
```

Q5 The program on the right is used to write birthday card messages.

Rewrite the program to match the output below. Use a single `print` function in your program.

```
age = input("Enter age: ")
print("Cheers to")
print(age)
print("years.")
print("And many more!")
```

```
Enter age: 15
Cheers to 15 years.
And many more!
```

Coding Challenges for Section Two

Here's your first set of coding challenges — each designed to apply the skills covered in this section. After you've had a bash, visit the link on the contents page to get example programs for each challenge.

Challenge 1 — Example

Create a program for a text adventure game. It should ask the player for their name and respond with their name and a piece of ASCII character art to represent an enemy, e.g.

```
 /)/)
( -|-)
c('')('')
```
A rabbit

SOLUTION

Plan: use input() to ask for the player's name and print() to display the response.

① The player's name is saved as the variable name.

```
name = input("Who dares enter my cavern? ")
print("Prepare for combat", name)
print(" /)/)\n( -|-)\nc('')('')")
```

```
Who dares enter my cavern? DemonDev
Prepare for combat DemonDev
 /)/)
( -|-)
c('')('')
```

② name is added to the printed message.

③ Brackets and slashes are used to create the character art. The new line escape character \n is used to separate lines.

Look back at p.14 if you need a reminder on using variables with input and print.

Challenge 2

You've been tasked with creating a program for a missing word game.

Your program should:
- Show a sentence with two missing words, e.g. "I love to put _____ on my _____"
- Ask for a word that could fill the first gap.
- Ask for a word that could fill the second gap.
- Repeat the sentence back to the user with their words filling the gaps.

Challenge 3

Box-Breaker Delivery have asked you to create a simple label maker program.

Your program should:
- Ask for the house number.
- Ask for the street name.
- Combine the house number and street name into one variable.
- Ask for the town.
- Ask for the postcode.
- Then display the whole address in the layout shown.

```
3 Challenge St.
Labelton
PY31 CGP
```

Challenge 4

Create a program that asks the user for three types of fruit beginning with specific letters. It should then repeat the fruits back to the user in one message and in alphabetical order.

Your program should:
- Ask for a fruit beginning with the letter S.
- Ask for a fruit beginning with the letter B.
- Ask for a fruit beginning with the letter P.
- Show the message:
  "In alphabetical order your fruits are _____, _____ and _____"

Hint: by placing the variables in alphabetical order when they are read back, it will appear to have sorted them.

Video Solution

Section Three — Data Types and Operators

Data Types

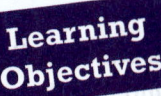

Is your data: text, a number, or something else entirely? To work correctly, Python relies on you giving it values of the correct data type.

- Learn about the <u>most common</u> data types in Python.
- Understand the need for different <u>data types</u> in programming.
- Learn that you can <u>convert</u> one data type to another.

There are four data types used in Python

You will find the following <u>data types</u> being used in this book:

String	Integer	Float	Boolean
Any <u>combination</u> of <u>letters</u>, <u>numbers</u> and <u>symbols</u>.	A positive or negative <u>whole number</u> (or zero). Decimal points <u>cannot</u> be used.	A number written with a <u>decimal point</u> — positive, negative or zero.	A <u>binary choice</u>: either <u>True</u> or <u>False</u>. (These are case sensitive.)
"You there?" "P@55w0rd!"	3827, -273	3.14, -98.0	True, False

Q1 What data types are the following values?
  a) -15.5   b) "False Answer"
  c) True   d) 2023

Case sensitive means that it matters which letters are capitalised. For example, 'True' is not the same as 'true'. Functions like print and input are also case sensitive — Print just won't work.

Python follows processing rules

1) Python needs to know what <u>type of data</u> it has to <u>process it correctly</u>.
2) Each data type has it's own <u>processing rules</u>. For example, you can use <u>integers</u> in <u>arithmetic calculations</u> (2 + 2 = 4), but that wouldn't work with <u>strings</u> ("two" + "two" = "twotwo" — see p.16)

You've already been adding quotes around words so Python knows they're strings.

Changing type changes behaviour

You sometimes need a <u>variable</u> to be a <u>specific data type</u>. These functions <u>convert</u> from one data type to another — this process is called <u>casting</u>.

Function	Converts to
str()	A string
int()	An integer
float()	A float

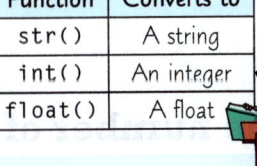

EXAMPLE Two programs written to add quiz scores (only one works as intended).

This version lets Python <u>assume</u> the data types.

```
round1 = input("Round 1: ")
round2 = input("Round 2: ")
quizScore = round1 + round2
print(quizScore)
```

Round 1: 4
Round 2: 5
45

The plus sign <u>concatenates</u> the scores because Python assumes all inputs are <u>strings</u>.

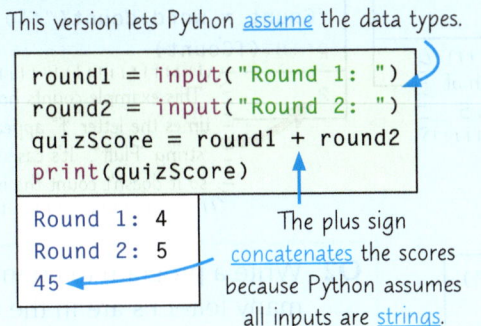

This version uses <u>casting</u> to convert to integers.

```
round1 = int(input("Round 1: "))
round2 = int(input("Round 2: "))
quizScore = round1 + round2
print(quizScore)
```

Round 1: 4
Round 2: 5
9

Each input() function is placed <u>inside</u> an int() function. This <u>casts</u> the input <u>string</u> to an <u>integer</u>.

The plus sign does the proper <u>addition</u> because the scores are now <u>integers</u>.

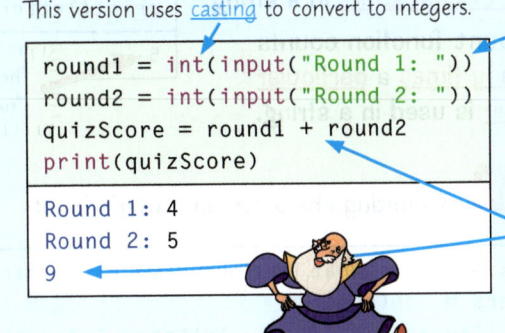

You don't *need* to wear wizard robes to cast, but I find it helps...

User inputs are treated as strings unless you convert them to another type. Mistakes with data types don't always cause error messages — the program might just do something silly instead.

How to Handle Strings

Learning Objectives

You may want to put on some gloves — you're about to be handling strings and I can't promise the user input will be clean. These pages show what you can do with strings.

- Understand the meaning of the term string handling.
- Be able to change the case of a string.
- Be able to count the characters in a string.
- Be able to identify a character by its position in a string.

String handling is about processing strings

1) A string is a collection of characters (letters, numbers or symbols) in any order.
2) Python has lots of ways that you can change strings or access parts of them.

The case of the letters can be changed

Imagine you are writing part of a game that contains upper and lower case text. For example, a person may be whispering in lowercase and shouting in uppercase.

EXAMPLE Here are two ways to change the case of a string.

A new variable is created for the changed text.

```
whisper = "CAN YOU HEAR ME?"
lowerWhisper = whisper.lower()
print(lowerWhisper)
```
```
can you hear me?
```

The symbols in the strings are not changed in any way, just the letters.

```
shout = "Look out!"
upperShout = shout.upper()
print(upperShout)
```
```
LOOK OUT!
```

.lower() or .upper() is added to the end of the original variable.

COMMON PROBLEMS Type quotation marks into IDLE yourself. If you copy and paste from other programs they won't always work.

Q1 Why doesn't this program print the text in upper case?

```
text = "take cover!"
upperText = text.upper()
print(text)
```
```
take cover!
```

The number of characters can be counted

- The `len` function counts the number of characters in a string.
- The `.count` function counts how many times a particular character is used in a string.

```
letters = len("toast")
print(letters)
```
```
5
```
The length of "toast" is 5.

```
word = "Fluff"
fCount = word.count("f")
print(fCount)
```
```
2
```
This example counts how many times the letter "f" appears in the string "Fluff". It's case sensitive, so it doesn't count the initial "F".

EXAMPLE Counting characters in a user's input.

```
snack = input("What is your favourite snack? ")
letters = len(snack)
print("Answer contains", letters, "characters")
```
```
What is your favourite snack? burnt toast
Answer contains 11 characters
```
It's 11 because the space is also a character.

Q2 Write a program to count how many letter r's are in the word "strawberry".

How to Handle Strings

Every character has an index position

1) If you want to find a character in a specific position in a string, you use an index.
2) In Python, you do this by putting the index in square brackets after the variable name.
3) You can find characters using positive indexes and negative indexes.

An **index** is a number that specifies a location of a character in a string.

Positive indexes begin at the start of a string

This table shows the positive index of each character in the string "chimpanzee".

Character	c	h	i	m	p	a	n	z	e	e
Index	0	1	2	3	4	5	6	7	8	9

It's easy to forget that 'positive' indexes start at 0, not 1.

EXAMPLE Identifying the first and last characters of a string.

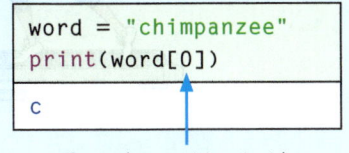

The index position inside square brackets identifies the first character at position 0.

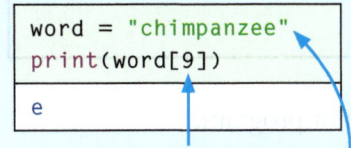

The index position inside square brackets identifies the last character at position 9.

Q3 Complete the output for the program below.

```
word = "chimpanzee"
print(word[5])
```

Negative indexes begin at the end of a string

1) Sometimes you need to count from the end of a string, especially if you don't know how long the string will be (e.g. if it comes from user input).
2) Negative indexes works like positive indexes but in reverse. They start at the end with the index position of –1.

Character	p	o	o	l		p	a	r	t	y
Index	–10	–9	–8	–7	–6	–5	–4	–3	–2	–1

Don't forget, the space between the two words is also a character.

EXAMPLE Identifying the first and last characters of a string.

```
text = "pool party"
print(text[-1])
```
y

The index position inside square brackets identifies the last character at position –1.

```
text = "pool party"
print(text[-10])
```
p

The index position inside square brackets identifies the first character at position –10.

Q4 Complete the output for the program below.

```
text = "pool party"
print(text[-4])
```

GOING FURTHER You can use **string slicing** to get part of a string, rather than a single character. E.g. try using `text[0:4]` in the program above.

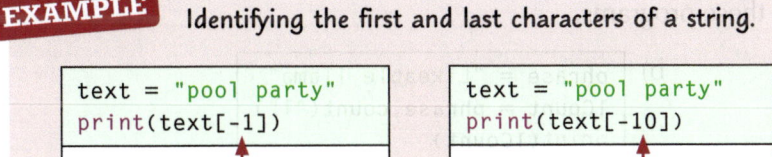

Python is kind enough to throw an error your way if you use an index outside the characters of a string, but drawing a table like the ones on this page can help prevent mistakes in the first place.

Section Three — Data Types and Operators

Practice Questions

Warm-Up

Q1 What is the purpose of using the `len` function on a string?

Q2 Which function can tell you how many times the letter 'u' appears in the word "tumultuous"?

Q3 What is the index position of the first character in a string?

Q4 Which character in a string has an index position of –1?

Practice Questions

Q1 Complete this data type table.

Data Type	Example
	True or False
Integer	
	"Think of a number"
Float	

Q2 A student has created a calculator program.

a) In order to add two user-inputted whole numbers, the strings need to be converted to which data type? ....

b) What is the name of this process? ....

Q3 Describe the two errors in the program below.

```
totalDistance = 100
distanceRun = str(input("How far have you run? "))
remainingDistance = totalDistance - distanceRun
print("Distance left is", remaining)
```

1. ....

2. ....

Q4 Complete the output for each of these programs.

a)
```
surname = "Lengthson"
print(len(surname))
```

b)
```
phrase = "Likeable llama"
lCount = phrase.count("l")
print(lCount)
```

Q5 A banking program has been designed to hide part of a username when sending emails.

Complete this program so that it displays the first and last letters of the username with six asterisks (*) in between.

```
username = input("Enter username: ")
first =
last =
print(                                    )
Enter username: catPants23
c******3
```

Working with Integers and Floats

Learning Objectives
As you create more complex programs you'll start to include simple calculations. Computers love doing the maths, so all you need to do is supply the code.
- Learn the four basic arithmetic operators.
- Be able to use integers and floats in simple calculations.

Integers and floats are used in calculations

1) Integers are whole numbers that are either positive, negative or zero.
2) Floats are also numbers, but they contain decimal points.

Do simple maths using arithmetic operators

Arithmetic operators are used to carry out basic mathematics — adding, subtracting, multiplying and dividing.

Arithmetic operator	+	-	*	/
What it's used for	Adding two numbers together	Subtracting one number from another	Multiplying two numbers	Dividing one number by another

EXAMPLE An example of each arithmetic operator in action.

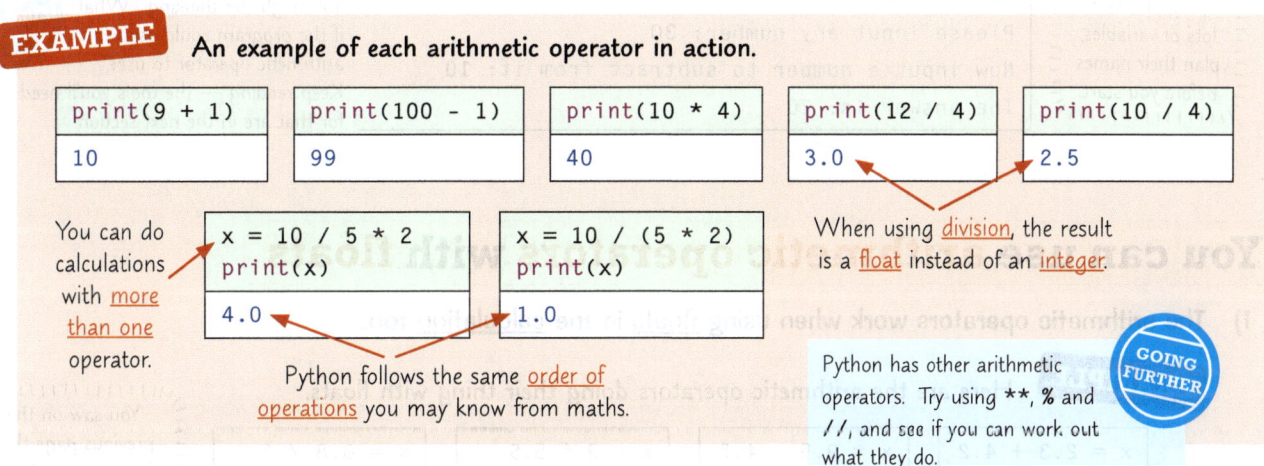

You can do calculations with more than one operator.

Python follows the same order of operations you may know from maths.

When using division, the result is a float instead of an integer.

Python has other arithmetic operators. Try using **, % and //, and see if you can work out what they do. *GOING FURTHER*

They also work with variables

EXAMPLE Here's how to calculate with variables.

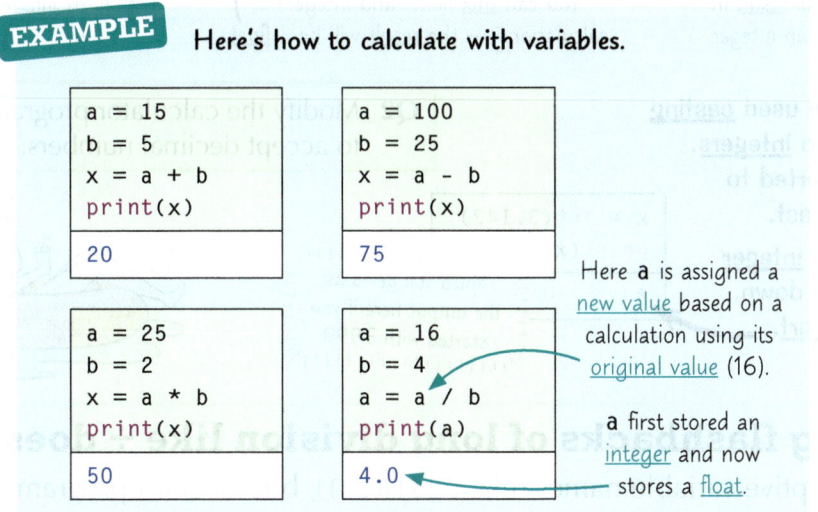

```
a = 15
b = 5
x = a + b
print(x)
```
20

```
a = 100
b = 25
x = a - b
print(x)
```
75

```
a = 25
b = 2
x = a * b
print(x)
```
50

```
a = 16
b = 4
a = a / b
print(a)
```
4.0

Here **a** is assigned a new value based on a calculation using its original value (16).

a first stored an integer and now stores a float.

Q1 Fill in the missing operator to create the output shown below.

```
a = 6
b = 4
x = a ...... b
print(x)
```
1.5

Section Three — Data Types and Operators

Working with Integers and Floats

Inputs + operators = a simple calculator

- You can build a calculator program by combining user input with arithmetic operators.
- This is the longest program you have seen so far but you've got this.

EXAMPLE A simple program that calculates with user input.

All inputs need to be converted to integers using casting.

Variables used in the same calculation have similar names. For example, these all begin with sub.

Pro tip: when creating a program with lots of variables, plan their names before you start.

```
print("Welcome to the Python Calculator Version 1.0")
add1 = int(input("Please input any number: "))
add2 = int(input("Tell me another number to add to it: "))
addTotal = add1 + add2
print("The answer is:", addTotal)
sub1 = int(input("Let's go again.\nPlease input any number: "))
sub2 = int(input("Now input a number to subtract from it: "))
subTotal = sub1 - sub2
print("The answer is:", subTotal)
```

```
Welcome to the Python Calculator Version 1.0
Please input any number: 50
Tell me another number to add to it: 10
The answer is: 60
Let's go again.
Please input any number: 30
Now input a number to subtract from it: 10
The answer is: 20
```

The escape character \n has been used to start a new line (see p.16).

Adding a space at the end of an input instruction makes it look neater when it appears in the output.

GOING FURTHER You might be thinking, "What if the program could ask which arithmetic operator to use?" Keep reading — the tools you'll need for that are in the next section.

You can use arithmetic operators with floats

1) The arithmetic operators work when using floats in the calculation too.

EXAMPLE Here are the arithmetic operators doing their thing with floats.

x = 2.3 + 4.2	x = 9.5 - 4.5	x = 2 * 5.5	x = 8.8 / 2
print(x)	print(x)	print(x)	print(x)
6.5	5.0	11.0	4.4

Calculations with floats will result in a float, even if it could be an integer.

You can mix floats and integers in calculations — the result will be a float.

You saw on the previous page that dividing two integers gives a float, but none of these operators will turn floats into integers.

2) The calculator program above used casting to convert the input strings to integers. You could instead have converted to floats by using float() to cast.

3) You can convert a float to an integer too — it doesn't round up or down, it just removes the decimal part.

```
x = int(3.142)
print(x)
3
```

You'd still get 3 as the output here if you started with 3.999.

Q2 Modify the calculator program above to accept decimal numbers.

Weird, / doesn't bring flashbacks of long division like ÷ does...

It's generally better to use descriptive variable names (like addTotal), but for short programs you can use simple ones like a, b and x — it's common practice (which means lots of people do it).

Section Three — Data Types and Operators

Practice Questions

Warm-Up

Q1 Which data type is used for numbers with a decimal point?

Q2 Why do you need to cast user inputs before doing a mathematical calculation with them?

Q3 What will be the value of x after this line of code? `x = 2.25 * 4`

Practice Questions

Q1 What data type will the result be if an integer is divided by another integer?

....

Q2 Explain the two errors in the table below.

Operation	Addition	Subtraction	Multiplication	Division
Symbol	+	-	×	\

1. ....

2. ....

Q3 Fill in the gaps to complete the programs below.

a)
```
a = 60
b = 4
c = a ..... b
print(c)
```
15.0

b)
```
a = 20
b = ............... - a
print(b)
```
80

c)
```
.....................
b = a + 48
print(b)
```
100

Q4 Complete the output for the following programs.

a)
```
a = 5 / 2.5
print(a)
```

b)
```
b = 1.1 * 9
print(b)
```

c)
```
c = int(0.22)
print(c)
```

d)
```
d = int(9.76)
print(d)
```

Relational Operators

Learning Objectives
Sometimes you want to compare two values to see if they're the same, or work out which is bigger or smaller. This is where relational operators are useful.
- Understand the need for relational operators.
- Learn the six most common relational operators.
- Be able to create a simple comparison program.

Relational operators compare values

1) A comparison will result in a True or False result.
2) There are many real world uses of relational operators — for example:
   - Video games — e.g. when comparing your score to the high score.
   - Social media apps — e.g. when comparing the number of views or likes.
   - Websites that restrict access to content based on your age.

In Section 4 you'll use relational operators to help make decisions.

Here are the ones you need to know

1) Below are six Python relational operators you need to know.
2) Each will result in a Boolean value — either True or False.
3) The first two (== and !=) are useful for comparing all data types. You will mainly use the other four with integers and floats.

Look back to p.19 for a reminder about the Boolean data type.

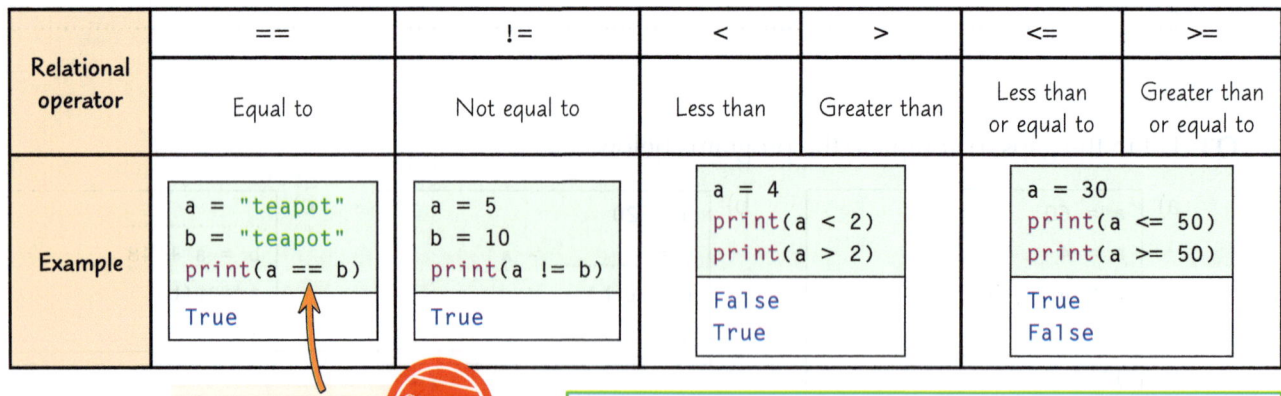

Relational operator	==	!=	<	>	<=	>=
	Equal to	Not equal to	Less than	Greater than	Less than or equal to	Greater than or equal to
Example	a = "teapot" b = "teapot" print(a == b) True	a = 5 b = 10 print(a != b) True	a = 4 print(a < 2) print(a > 2) False True		a = 30 print(a <= 50) print(a >= 50) True False	

COMMON PROBLEMS: If you use one = sign instead of two here, it will cause an error.

Q1 Change the value of a in each example in the table to create the opposite results to the ones shown.

EXAMPLE
You can use relational operators to make a yes/no decision.

The user input is converted to an integer so that it can be compared.

```
print("You must score 90 or above to proceed.")
passScore = 90
userScore = int(input("Enter your score: "))
print("Can you proceed?", userScore >= passScore)
```

The greater than or equal to operator is used to compare the user score to the pass score.

```
You must score 90 or above to proceed.
```

A score of 89 is not high enough so the user can't proceed.

```
Enter your score: 89
Can you proceed? False
```
```
Enter your score: 90
Can you proceed? True
```

A score of 90 is equal to the pass score so the user can proceed.

Score 90 to pass? What a coincidence, that's exactly what I got...

Maths has one equals sign (=), so why does Python need two (==)? It's because they do different things. Python uses = to assign values to variables and == to compare them. That's just how it is.

Section Three — Data Types and Operators

Boolean Operators

Learning Objectives

Nearly done — just one more set of operators to cover. Boolean logic is at the core of computing and there are multiple ways to build it into your programs.

- Understand the need for Boolean operators.
- Learn the three most common Boolean operators.
- Be able to combine Boolean and relational operators.

Boolean operators work with Boolean values

1) Sometimes you need to check the result of more than one comparison at once — for example, checking a number is between two limits, or allowing multiple correct answers to a question.
2) Boolean operators let you take Boolean values (True or False) and output another Boolean value based on some rules.

GOING FURTHER — Learn more about Boolean logic and how it relates to binary (1s and 0s) to understand why computers are so darn good at it.

Boolean operator	and	or	not
How it works	If both variables are True, then the output is True, otherwise the output is False.	If either variable is True, then the output is True, otherwise the output False.	If the variable is True, then the output is opposite — False. Likewise, False becomes True.

EXAMPLE Here's how each Boolean operator is used.

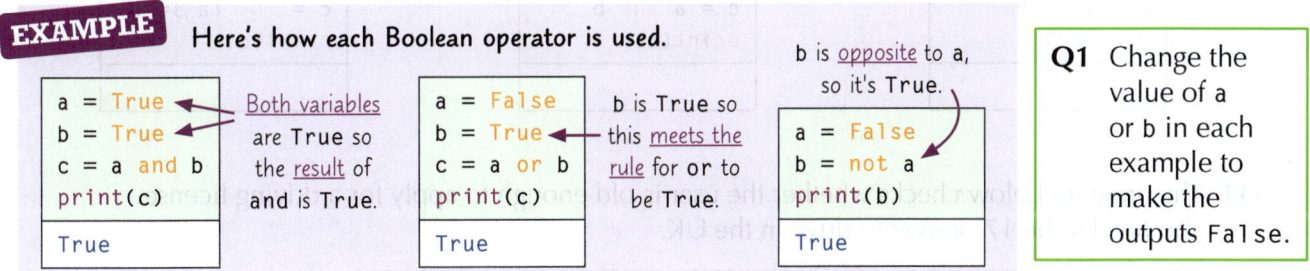

Q1 Change the value of a or b in each example to make the outputs False.

You can combine Boolean and relational operators

EXAMPLE How a two-player game could check that both players meet the age requirements.

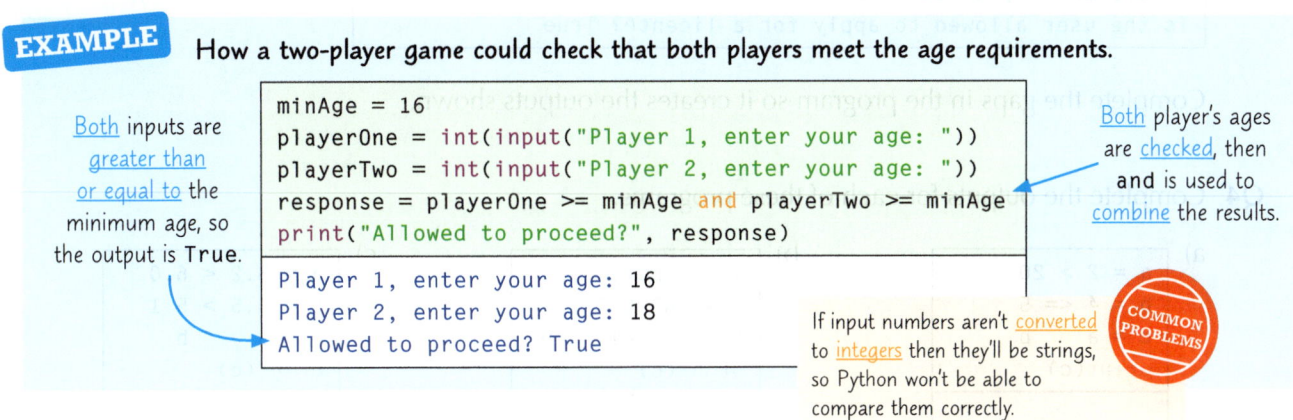

Both inputs are greater than or equal to the minimum age, so the output is True.

Both player's ages are checked, then and is used to combine the results.

COMMON PROBLEMS — If input numbers aren't converted to integers then they'll be strings, so Python won't be able to compare them correctly.

Boo! Ahem, sorry, let me start again — Boolean operators...

You've now seen all the main Python operators that'll be used in this book. The Boolean operators are all written as words, so they're easy to tell apart from the arithmetic and relational ones.

Section Three — Data Types and Operators

Practice Questions

Warm-Up

Q1 Which relational operator represents 'Less than or equal to'?

Q2 Name the three basic Boolean operators.

Q3 Which Boolean operator only outputs `True` when both inputs are `True`?

Q4 Which Boolean operator outputs the opposite value to its input?

Practice Questions

Q1 Draw a line matching each relational operator to the correct description.

- `==` — Not equal to
- `>=` — Equal to
- `!=` — Less than
- `<` — Greater than or equal to

Q2 Complete the outputs for each of these programs.

a)
```
a = False
b = False
c = a or b
print(c)
```

b)
```
a = not False
b = True
c = a and b
print(c)
```

c)
```
a = True
b = True
c = not (a != b)
print(c)
```

Q3 The program below checks whether the user is old enough to apply for a driving license. You need to be 17 or over to drive in the UK.

```
age = int(input("Please enter your age: "))
drivingAge = 17
.................... = age ............ ........................
print("Is the user allowed to apply for a licence?", licence)
```
```
Please enter your age: 18
Is the user allowed to apply for a licence? True
```

Complete the gaps in the program so it creates the outputs shown.

Q4 Complete the outputs for each of these programs.

a)
```
a = 2 > 20
b = 4 <= 5
c = a or b
print(c)
```

b)
```
a = "apple"
b = "APPLE"
c = not (a == b)
print(c)
```

c)
```
a = 3.2 < 6.0
b = 4.5 > 5.1
c = a and b
print(c)
```

Section Three — Data Types and Operators

Coding Challenges for Section Three

How much has sunk in? Let's find out — it's time to test what you've learnt in this section. Have a go at these coding challenges, and then visit the link on the contents page for example programs for each one.

Challenge 1 — Example

You have been asked to create an animal quiz in which players guess the name of an animal with a certain number of letters. The host of the game asking the questions is called Joolean.

Your program should:
- Have the game host introduce themselves to the player.
- Ask the player to name an animal with four letters that starts with the letter b.
- Change the case of the player's input to lowercase.
- Display the statement "Does your guess fit both rules?" followed by True or False.

SOLUTION Plan: use string handling and Boolean logic to check the player's guess.

① The response in converted to lowercase.

③ The number of letters is counted.

④ The relational operator == is used to test each rule.

```
print("Woof woof, my name is Joolean!")
print("Name an animal with 4 letters, starting with b.")
guess = input("What is your guess? ")
lowerGuess = guess.lower()
firstLetter = lowerGuess[0]
letters = len(guess)
response = firstLetter == "b" and letters == 4
print("Does your guess fit both rules?", response)
```

② The first letter (with index position 0) is stored.

⑤ The Boolean operator and is used to check that both rules are followed.

```
Woof woof, my name is Joolean!
Name an animal with 4 letters, starting with b.
What is your guess? Bear
Does your guess fit both rules? True
```

Challenge 2

Create a simple lottery game that asks the user to guess two numbers between 1 and 50 (inclusive). These need to be compared to the winning numbers and if both are the same then they win!

Video Solution

Your program should:
- Store two winning numbers (e.g. 15 and 32).
- Explain the rules to the user.
- Ask the user to input each of their two guesses, in numerical order.
- Check if the user's guesses match the winning numbers.
- Display the statement "Have you won this week?" followed by True or False.

For an extra challenge, use Boolean logic to make the program work if the numbers are entered in any order.

Challenge 3

An electric vehicle company is experimenting with speed calculators. You have been asked to create a program that calculates the average speed over a set distance and compare this to the speed limit.

Your program should:
- Ask for the speed limit in km/h (kilometres per hour).
- Ask for the distance travelled in kilometres.
- Ask for the time in hours taken to travel that distance.
- Calculate the average speed in km/h by dividing the distance travelled by the time taken.
- Output the average speed and a message saying "Has the speed limit been broken?", followed by True or False.

Section Four — Selection

Selection

Learning Objectives

Shall I do this? Or shall I do that? Life is all about these tough choices and programming is no different. But don't fear, Python is equipped to handle it.

- Learn about the three types of blocks used in programming.
- Understand the purpose of selection statements.
- Learn about the types of programs that use selection.
- Understand how selection can be visualised in a flowchart.

Programs are built in blocks

A block in programming is a section of related code.

There are three types of blocks that programmers use.
1) **Sequence** — logical step-by-step code that runs line by line from top to bottom.
2) **Selection** — has multiple paths and can react to user input and variables.
3) **Iteration** — uses loops to repeat actions as many times as needed.

All the examples you've seen so far used sequence. Iteration is covered in Sections 5 and 6.

Selection statements make choices

There are many examples of how selection can be used in programs.
- To display different responses for different user inputs.
- To change the path a program takes based on user input.
- To make decisions based on the value of variables.

Flowcharts are a good way to visualise selection

EXAMPLE Here's a simple question we all know the answer to (don't we?).

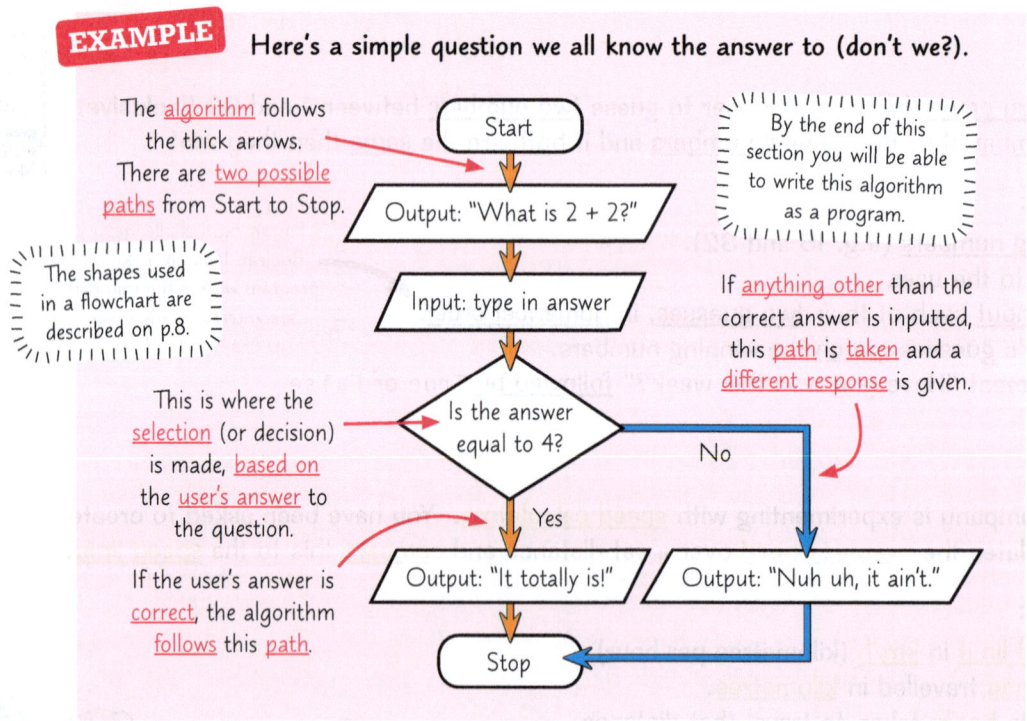

The algorithm follows the thick arrows. There are two possible paths from Start to Stop.

The shapes used in a flowchart are described on p.8.

This is where the selection (or decision) is made, based on the user's answer to the question.

If the user's answer is correct, the algorithm follows this path.

By the end of this section you will be able to write this algorithm as a program.

If anything other than the correct answer is inputted, this path is taken and a different response is given.

Q1 Sketch a flowchart for a program that asks "Do cats wear pants?" and responds to the answer.

Input: please enter some witty banter, our writer is on holiday...

Flowcharts are a great way to present algorithms that involve selection — you can see the multiple paths and possible outcomes. As you'll find out soon, they're easily converted to Python.

if Statements

Learning Objectives

Once you bring choices and selection into your programs, they'll get proper good. So let's not dilly-dally any longer — it's time to master the art of decision-making.

- Understand the purpose of if statements.
- Learn the structure and syntax of an if statement.
- Be able to include relational and Boolean operators in conditions.

if statements are used to make decisions

1) You use "if" to make decisions in everyday life, e.g. "If it's raining, I'll take an umbrella."
2) Python and many other programming languages use if statements in a similar way.

EXAMPLE Using an if statement to create part of the flowchart on the previous page.

This says: if the condition "answer equals 4" is True, then carry out the indented lines below.

```
answer = input("What is 2 + 2? ")
if answer == "4":
    print("It totally is!")
print("Thanks for your answer.")
```

The colon is needed at the end of the condition.

Any indented lines are only carried out if the condition is True.

The output is different depending on the answer given.

```
What is 2 + 2? 4
It totally is!
Thanks for your answer.
```

```
What is 2 + 2? 5
Thanks for your answer.
```

The if statement ends when the code is no longer indented, so this line is always carried out.

Remember, == (not =) means 'equal to' (p.26).

Indentation is part of the syntax rules

- An indent is a gap at the start of a line of code.
- IDLE will automatically add an indent if you press the Return key after typing the colon in an if statement.
- You can use the Tab key to add indents yourself.

Missing the colon or indent will cause a syntax error in your program.  **COMMON PROBLEMS**

You can include operators in conditions

Look back at p.26-27 for a recap on relational and Boolean operators.

EXAMPLE Using operators to make more complex decisions.

```
print("You must be 16 or over to play.")
age = int(input("How old are you? "))
if age >= 16:
    print("Enjoy the game")
```

```
You must be 16 or over to play.
How old are you? 99999
Enjoy the game
```

The condition is only met if age is greater than or equal to 16.

```
username = input("Enter username: ")
password = input("Enter password: ")
if username == "luke" and password == "cat":
    print("Access granted")
```

```
Enter username: luke
Enter password: cat
Access granted
```

Both username and password must be correct for the condition to be True.

OK so I just indented an excuse to make this joke...

Python is quite fussy about indentation — it'll usually scream about syntax errors if you get it wrong. This is also the case for the other types of statements you'll see later in this book.

Practice Questions

Warm-Up

Q1 Name the three types of blocks used in programming.

Q2 What word describes a block of code that runs line by line, top to bottom?

Q3 What shape represents a decision in a flowchart?

Q4 What is wrong with this line of code? `if speed = 70:`

Practice Questions

Q1 Explain the purpose of a selection statement.

....

....

Q2 Circle and describe the two errors in the program below.

```
temp = int(input("Enter a temperature that would freeze water: "))
if temp >= 0:
print("Correct, well done.")
```

1. ....

2. ....

Q3 Complete the output for the following two programs.

a)
```
batteryCharge = 15
if batteryCharge < 10:
    print("Warning — battery low!!")
print("% remaining:", batteryCharge)
```

b)
```
guessedWord = "turkey"
if guessedWord != "octopus":
    print("Obviously not!")
print("Thanks for playing")
```

Q4 Describe two syntax rules that need to be followed when using an `if` statement.

1. ....

2. ....

Q5 Complete the gaps in the program below so it displays the output shown.

```
1    print("Which two numbers can 7 be divided by without remainders?")
2    number1 = input("Enter the smaller number: ")
3    ....................................................................................................
4    if number1 == "1" .............. number2 .......... ..............
5        print("Correct")
```
```
Which two numbers can 7 be divided by without remainders?
Enter the smaller number: 1
Enter the larger number: 7
Correct
```

In this program, the input is left as a string. You would need to cast to integers if you wanted to do arithmetic or compare using < or >, etc.

Section Four — Selection

The else Clause

Learning Objectives

No offence, but your selection blocks are still a bit puny. Sometimes responding to a wrong answer is as important as responding to the right one. Here's how.

- Understand the purpose of an else clause.
- Be able to use an else clause in an if statement.

Use else to catch wrong answers

1) In previous examples, when the condition of an if statement wasn't True the program just moved on to the next unindented line of code.
2) You can use else to provide an option for when the condition is False.
3) else is referred to as a clause and it can't be used on its own — it's only used as an optional part of an if statement.

EXAMPLE Programming the flow chart on p.30 again — this time allowing for wrong answers.

This line of code is only carried out when a correct answer creates a True condition.

A wrong answer creates a False condition and triggers the else clause, meaning this line of code is carried out instead.

```
answer = input("What is 2 + 2? ")
if answer == "4":
    print("It totally is!")
else:
    print("Nuh uh, it ain't.")
print("Thanks for your answer.")
```
```
What is 2 + 2? 22
Nuh uh, it ain't.
Thanks for your answer.
```
```
What is 2 + 2? 4
It totally is!
Thanks for your answer.
```

Another colon is needed here, as well as the indent below it.

This line will always run whether the condition was True or False.

 **GOING FURTHER**

If you're thinking, "Why not give the user another go when they get it wrong?", Section 6 will help you with that.

Use 'or' to allow multiple answers

EXAMPLE Any one of three possible answers can be given in this program.

```
day = input("Name a day of the week that has six letters: ")
if day == "monday" or day == "friday" or day == "sunday":
    print("Correct, that's one of the three.")
else:
    print("Not quite friend, not quite.")
```
```
Name a day of the week that has six letters. sunday
Correct, that's one of the three.
```

The Boolean operator or is used between each possible answer.

'monday', 'friday' or 'sunday' are all accepted as correct answers.

Any other answer is handled by the else clause.

Q1 Add a new line of code that uses a string handling function so that capitalised answers such as 'Sunday' are accepted.

A full expression, including the variable, needs to be put between every or. You can't do something like:
`if day == "monday" or "friday":`
That won't work properly.

 **COMMON PROBLEMS**

I'm tellin' ya, you gotta learn this stuff, or else...

Always try to think about the different ways a user might respond to a question. E.g. they might use the wrong CasE or spell a word wrogn. Programmers try to allow for this (within reason).

Section Four — Selection

The elif Clause

Learning Objectives

There's one more upgrade to the `if` statement before you unlock its ultimate power. Not every decision is black and white — sometimes there are many cases to deal with.

- Understand the purpose of the `elif` clause.
- Be able to use an `elif` clause in an `if` statement.

elif allows for multiple responses

elif is short for 'else if'.

1) An `elif` clause is another optional part of an `if` statement.
2) It can be used to check another condition if the first one was `False`.
3) More than one `elif` clause can be used in the same `if` statement. The conditions are checked in order until one is found to be `True`.
4) You can still include an `else` clause for when all conditions are `False`.

EXAMPLE Here's a new and improved chatbot like the ones from Section 2. This one wants to know your opinion on the latest superhero film.

```
print("It's me, CGPbot 3")
print("So how'd you like the movie?")
stars = input("Enter one (*) to three (***) stars: ")
if stars == "*":
    print("Yikes, I'll give it a miss!")
elif stars == "**":
    print("Average? I'll wait to stream it.")
elif stars == "***":
    print("Wow, I'll check it out!")
elif stars == "mango":
    print("Initiating Operation Mango...")
else:
    print("Come on now, I said one to three stars.")
print("CGPbot out")
```

The `if` condition is put first and is always checked.

Each `elif` condition is only checked if the condition above it was `False`.

The `else` clause must be put last after the `if` and `elif`s.

`if` and `elif` are used to check each user response separately, so that a different response can be given for each.

The `else` clause is used to respond to any other input from the user.

```
It's me, CGPbot 3
So how'd you like the movie?
Enter one (*) to three (***) stars: **
Average? I'll wait to stream it.
CGPbot out
```

Here `stars` is not equal to `"*"` so the `if` condition is `False`.

The first `elif` condition is then checked and found to be `True`, so that clause is used.

Once one clause has been used, the rest of the conditions are skipped.

```
Enter one (*) to three (***) stars: ***
Wow, I'll check it out!
CGPbot out
```

Here the `if` and first `elif` condition are checked in order and both found to be `False`.

The second `elif` condition is `True`, so that one is used.

Q1 Complete the next line of output for the input shown.

```
Enter one (*) to three (***) stars: ****
```

Remember all the relephant facts — elif fans never forget...

Multiple `elif` clauses can be used in the same `if` statement, but there should only be one `if` at the start and (at most) one `else` at the end. So go nuts — use as many `elif`s as you want!

Section Four — Selection

Practice Questions

Warm-Up

Q1 Which operator can be used to check for multiple correct answers in one `if` statement?

Q2 Which clause can be used to check additional conditions in an `if` statement?

Q3 How should code inside an `if`, `elif` or `else` clause be formatted?

Q4 What is wrong with this order of statements: `if, elif, else, elif`?

Practice Questions

Q1 Tick whether the following statements are True or False.

Statement	True	False
An `else` clause is carried out when the `if` statement's condition is `True`.		
A maximum of three `elif` clauses can be used in an `if` statement.		
Only one `else` clause can be used in an `if` statement.		

Q2 There are two errors in the program below.

```
1  digit = int(input("Enter a single-digit multiple of 4: "))
2  if digit == 4 or digit == 8:
3      print("Yep, that's right.")
4  else digit == 0 or digit == -4 or digit == -8:
5      print("You're a clever one ain't ya?")
6  else
7      print("That ain't right, sorry.")
```

No Python, just vibes

a) Circle and describe the errors.

1. ....

2. ....

b) Rewrite the lines with errors to resolve them.

Q3 The program below gives an award based on the user's score. Complete the program using the score boundaries in the table.

Award	Points
Bronze	10-19
Silver	20-29
Gold	30+

```
1  score = int(input("Please enter your score: "))
2  if score ......... ..................:
3      print("Gold award — spectacular!")
4  elif score ......... ..................:
5      print("Silver award — brill!")
6  elif score ......... ..................:
7      print("Bronze award — well it's something!")
8  else:
9      print("Better luck next time...")
```

Hint: remember, `elif` conditions are only checked if the previous conditions are all false. E.g. if the code gets to line 4, you already know the score must be less than the boundary for the gold reward.

Section Four — Selection

Coding Challenges for Section Four

We're really building up steam now, but let's do another set of challenges before going on to the next section. Give them your best shot, then visit the link on the contents page to get example programs for each challenge.

Challenge 1 — Example

Create a maths quiz that states a number and asks the user for a number that it's divisible by. It should respond with a message telling them whether they were right or wrong.

SOLUTION Plan: use an `if` statement with an `else` clause to create a selection block with a right path and a wrong path.

① The input is stored as an integer so it can be processed.

```
n = int(input("Enter a number that 18 is divisible by: "))
if n == 1 or n == 2 or n == 3 or n == 6 or n == 9 or n == 18:
    print("Correct, 18 is divisible by", n)
else:
    print("Sorry, incorrect answer.")
```

② The Boolean operator `or` is used to check all the possible answers.

```
Enter any number that is 18 divisible by? 9
Correct, 18 is divisible by 9
```

③ If none of the possible answers are inputted, the `else` clause shows the 'incorrect' message.

Challenge 2

Write a program for a smart speaker that makes footwear suggestions based on the weather.

Your program should:
- Ask the user their name, and whether it's sunny, cloudy or raining outside.
- Reply with a message containing the user's name and a suitable footwear suggestion (e.g. sandals, trainers or wellies).

Challenge 3

A banking app asks users to confirm their username and two digits in their password before it will open.

Write a program that will:
- Store a sample username and password (at least 6 characters long).
- Ask the user for their username.
- Ask the user for the 3rd and 6th character of their password.
- Check the name and password characters match the stored values.
- Tell the user whether they can proceed or that their details were incorrect.

Remember that string index positions start at 0 — see p.21 for more.

Challenge 4

Create a game where the player must guess a number from 1 to 100 (including 1 and 100). If they guess correctly they win, otherwise they're told whether their number is too high or too low.

Your program should:
- Store an integer between 1 and 100.
- Ask the user to guess the number.
- Compare the stored and guessed values.
- Display an appropriate message, e.g. "You win!", "Too high" or "Too low".
- (Optional) If they guessed wrong, display "Did you get within 10?" followed by `True` or `False`.

Until you learn to use `while` loops in Section 6, the user will have to restart the program to have another guess.

Video Solution

Challenge 5

Improve the calculator program on p.24 by allowing the user to input the operator they want to use (either +, -, * or /) and then showing the answer of the correct calculation.

Section Five — Iteration

Iteration

Learning Objectives

Your programs so far haven't run the same line of code more than once. Iteration adds loops to the mix with the ability to repeat code again, and again, and again.
- Understand the purpose of iteration.
- Be able to visualise iteration in a flowchart.

Iteration is used to repeat instructions

1) The sequence programs in Sections 2 & 3 all ran from top to bottom (line 1, then line 2, etc.) with every line of code being carried out once.
2) In Section 4, you used selection in programs to skip or run lines of code based on decisions, but each line was still carried out at most once.
3) Iteration is used to repeat a block of code a number of times. This means lines of code will be carried out more than once.
4) Using iteration in code is not only faster to write, but easier to change and fix (see the next page).

Go back to p.30 for a reminder about the different types of blocks in programming.

Flowcharts can use iteration

A common use of iteration is to repeat an action until a condition becomes true.

EXAMPLE A fairground ride cannot start until 4 passengers are seated. Here's how iteration could be used to control the start of the ride.

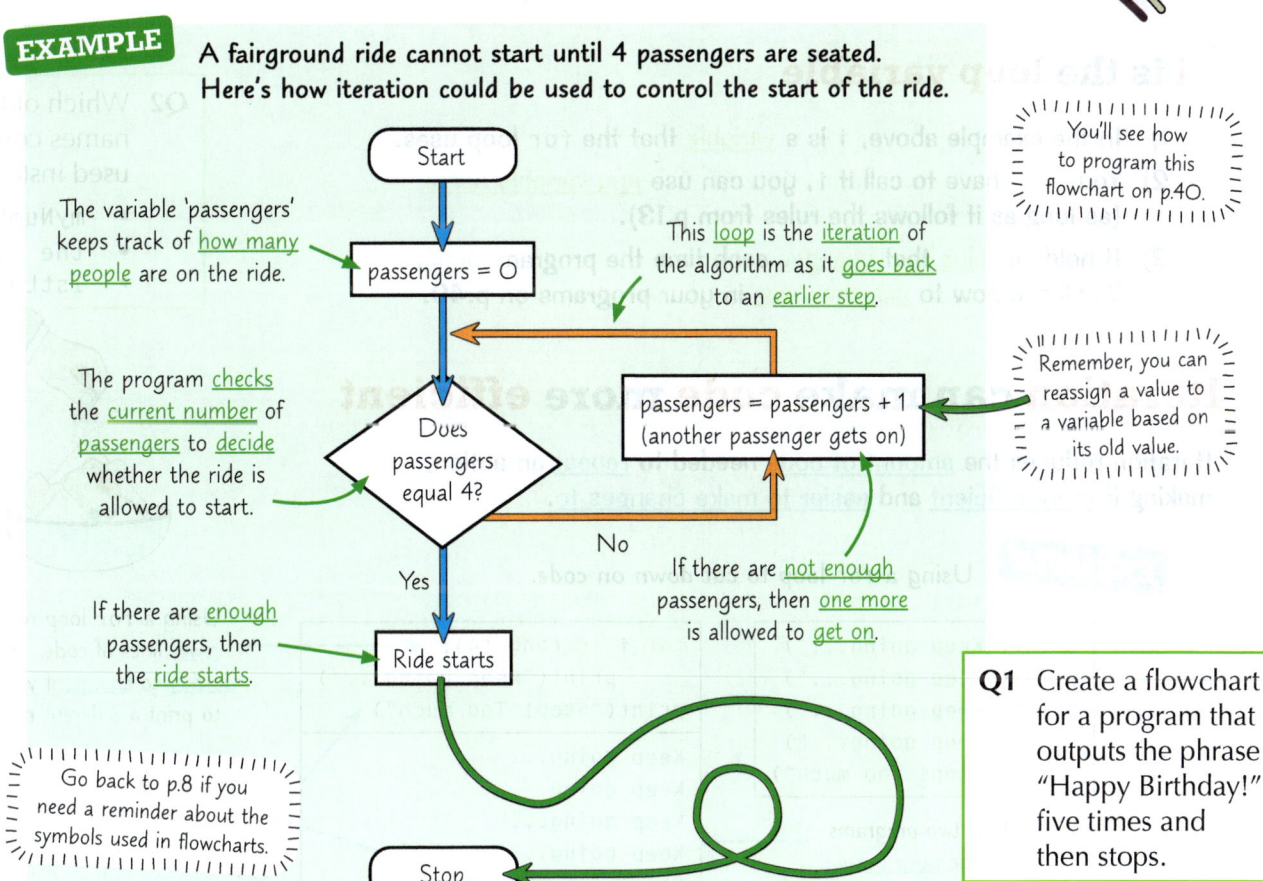

The variable 'passengers' keeps track of how many people are on the ride.

This loop is the iteration of the algorithm as it goes back to an earlier step.

The program checks the current number of passengers to decide whether the ride is allowed to start.

You'll see how to program this flowchart on p.40.

Remember, you can reassign a value to a variable based on its old value.

If there are not enough passengers, then one more is allowed to get on.

If there are enough passengers, then the ride starts.

Go back to p.8 if you need a reminder about the symbols used in flowcharts.

Q1 Create a flowchart for a program that outputs the phrase "Happy Birthday!" five times and then stops.

I hope you're excited about iteration, because I'm loopy for it...

It's a little easier to visualise iteration with flowcharts than it is in Python code (as you'll see soon). Make sure they're a part of your planning arsenal, alongside that stash of biscuits in your drawer.

for Loops

Learning Objectives: Enough flowcharts — how do you actually do iteration in your programs? Good question, if I say so myself. Python has a couple of answers, and the first is the humble for loop.
- Understand the purpose of a for loop.
- Learn the structure and syntax of a basic for loop.
- Be able to use a for loop to repeat code a number of times.

for loops repeat code a number of times

KEY TERMS: Iterate, loop and repeat all mean the same thing.

EXAMPLE Here's how the most basic for loop is done.

Ignore i for now, it will be explained later.

The indented code will be carried out every time the program loops.

The loop runs twice, so the messages are output twice.

```
for i in range(2):
    print("Echo!")
    print("!ohcE")
```

```
Echo!
!ohcE
Echo!
!ohcE
```

The number inside the range() sets how many times the code will loop.

COMMON PROBLEMS: Missing the colon or indent will cause a syntax error, just like the if statements on p.31.

Q1 Complete this program to create the output shown.

```
for i in range(....):
    ........("Ho!")
```

```
Ho!
Ho!
Ho!
```

i is the loop variable

1) In the example above, i is a variable that the for loop uses.
2) You don't have to call it i, you can use any variable name (as long as it follows the rules from p.13).
3) It holds a value that changes each time the program loops. You'll see how to use the value in your programs on p.40.

Q2 Which of these names could be used instead of i?
- myNumber
- the counter
- 1stLoop

Iteration can make code more efficient

Iteration reduces the amount of code needed to repeat an action, making it more efficient and easier to make changes to.

EXAMPLE Using a for loop to cut down on code.

```
print("Keep going...")
print("Keep going...")
print("Keep going...")
print("Keep going...")
print("Stop! Too much")
```

```
for i in range(4):
    print("Keep going...")
print("Stop! Too much")
```

```
Keep going...
Keep going...
Keep going...
Keep going...
Stop! Too much
```

These two programs have the same output.

Using a for loop results in fewer lines of code. It's also quicker to change if you decide to print a different message.

The last line is not indented, so it runs after the loop and isn't repeated.

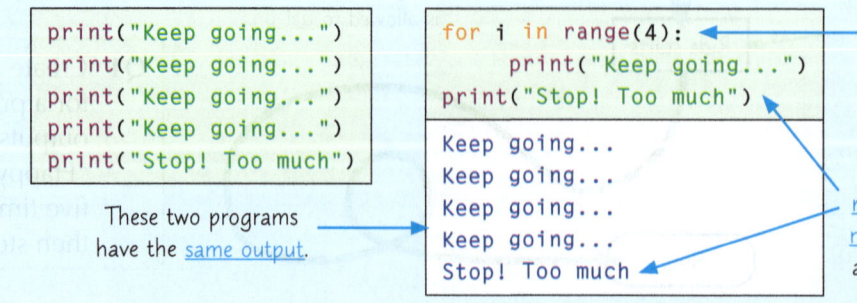

Am i derangeed or what? i can't see the forest for the trees...

Okay so yeah, the example above only saved us a few lines of code, but imagine if you needed to do something complex over 100 times — without iteration, that would be a copy-paste nightmare.

Practice Questions

Warm-Up

Q1 What feature of a flowchart shows that an algorithm uses iteration?

Q2 True or false? The loop variable in a `for` loop could be given any valid variable name.

Q3 What character is required at the end of the first line of a `for` loop?

Practice Questions

Q1 Describe what iteration is used for.

....

....

Q2 The following code snippets each contain an error. Find the error and explain why it occurs.

a)
```
for i in range(5):
print("Is there anybody there?")
```

....

b)
```
for i in range("ten"):
    print("Error!")
```

....

Q3 Complete the output for the following programs.

a)
```
for i in range(3):
    print("Get ready...")
print("Go!")
```

b)
```
for i in range(2):
    print("Hop forward")
    print("Step right")
```

Q4 Write a program that uses a `for` loop to create the output shown.

```
For she's a jolly good fellow
For she's a jolly good fellow
For she's a jolly good fellow
And so say all of us!
```

Q5 Explain one way in which using iteration can improve code.

....

....

Printing Numbers and Letters

Learning Objectives

This next bit is mostly about counting up and down. I think you'll be OK, but if you're struggling, feel free to use the page numbers of this book for reference.

- Understand how the value of the loop variable can be used in a for loop.
- Learn how to use start, stop and step values with the range function.
- Be able to create number sequences counting up and down.
- Be able to iterate through the letters in a string.

range() generates a sequence of numbers

You can use a for loop with the range function to count up from 0.

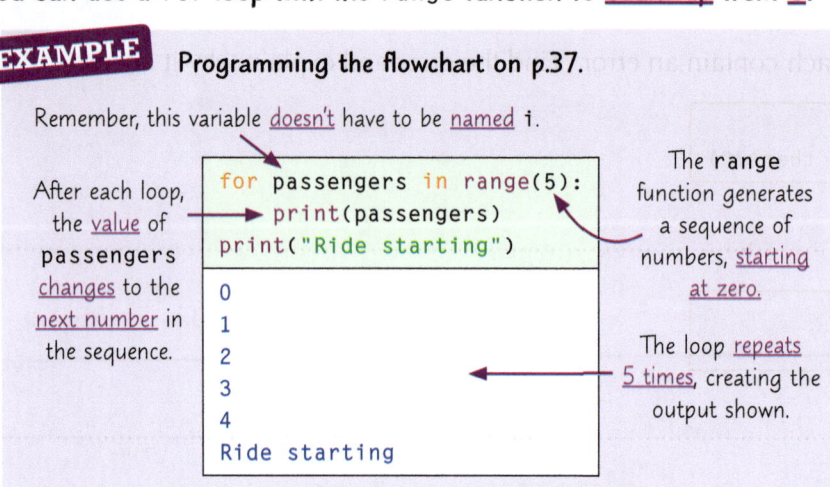

EXAMPLE Programming the flowchart on p.37.

Remember, this variable doesn't have to be named i.

After each loop, the value of passengers changes to the next number in the sequence.

```
for passengers in range(5):
    print(passengers)
print("Ride starting")
0
1
2
3
4
Ride starting
```

The range function generates a sequence of numbers, starting at zero.

The loop repeats 5 times, creating the output shown.

Q1 How would the output change if '5' was replaced by '2' in this example?

COMMON PROBLEMS — The sequence of numbers starts at 0. If you forget, then you might wonder why you're getting numbers one below what you wanted.

Q2 What is the error in the program below?

```
for j in range[5]:
    print(j)
```

You can change the start value

1) The above example used one number with range() — it represented the stop number.
2) You can also use two numbers with range(). The first will then be the start number, and the second will be the stop number.
3) This lets you count up between any pair of numbers.

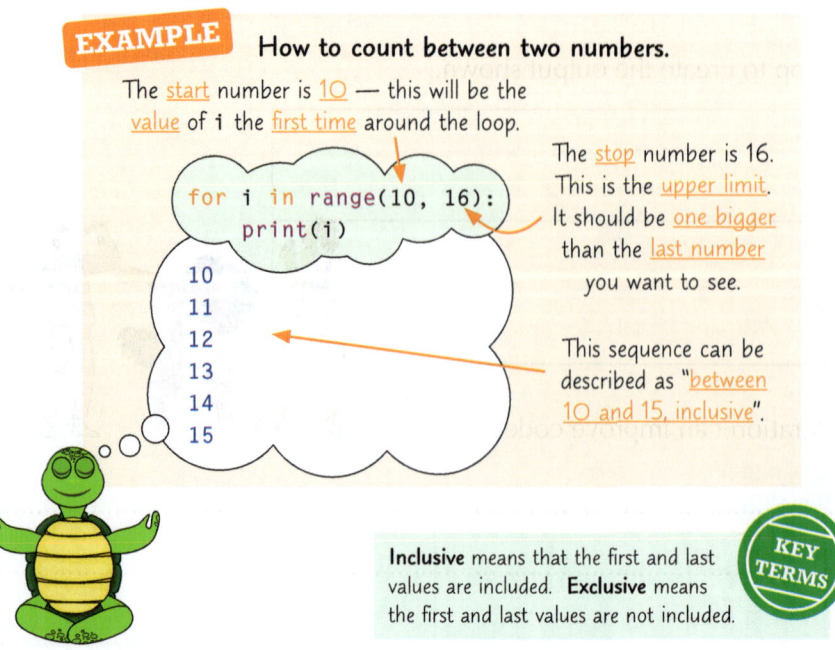

EXAMPLE How to count between two numbers.

The start number is 10 — this will be the value of i the first time around the loop.

```
for i in range(10, 16):
    print(i)
10
11
12
13
14
15
```

The stop number is 16. This is the upper limit. It should be one bigger than the last number you want to see.

This sequence can be described as "between 10 and 15, inclusive".

COMMON PROBLEMS — The loop ends when the value of i reaches the stop number. The code inside the loop won't be run for this value of i — the last value it sees will be one less.

Q3 Complete the output for the program below.

```
for i in range(7, 11):
    print(i)
```

KEY TERMS — **Inclusive** means that the first and last values are included. **Exclusive** means the first and last values are not included.

Section Five — Iteration

Printing Numbers and Letters

You can also change the step value

1) So far you've seen range() generate numbers that increase in steps of 1.
2) You can change this step value by giving range() a third number.

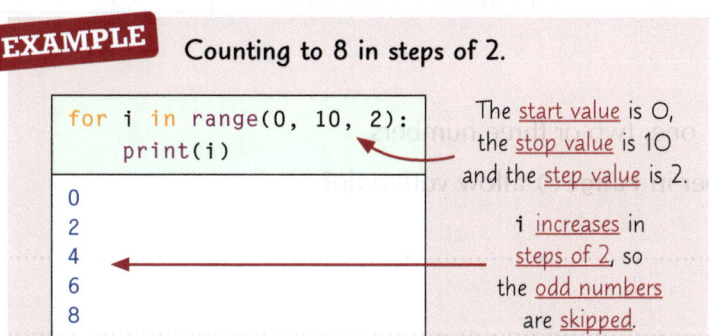

EXAMPLE Counting to 8 in steps of 2.

```
for i in range(0, 10, 2):
    print(i)
```
```
0
2
4
6
8
```

The start value is 0, the stop value is 10 and the step value is 2.

i increases in steps of 2, so the odd numbers are skipped.

Q4 Check out my program below.

```
for i in range(20, 81, 30):
    print(i)
```

a) Fill in the gaps:
   20 is the .... value,
   81 is the .... value,
   30 is the .... value.

b) Complete the output of the program.

3) If the step value is not 1, the loop will stop repeating when the loop variable is equal to or goes beyond the stop value. E.g. using range(0, 9, 2) in the example above will give the same output — after 8, i becomes 10 which is greater than the stop value.

4) You can give a negative step value to count down.

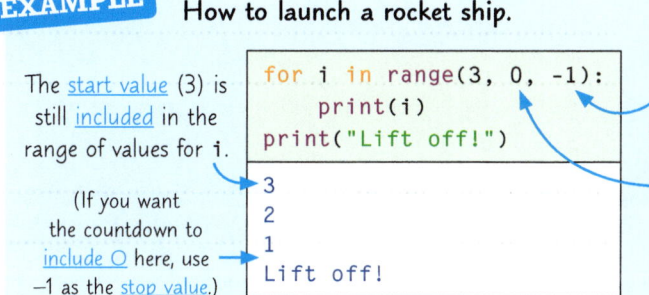

EXAMPLE How to launch a rocket ship.

The start value (3) is still included in the range of values for i.

(If you want the countdown to include 0 here, use −1 as the stop value.)

```
for i in range(3, 0, -1):
    print(i)
print("Lift off!")
```
```
3
2
1
Lift off!
```

A negative step value will decrease the value of i after each iteration.

As i is decreasing, the stop value should be less than the start value.

Iterate through a string one character at a time

- You can use a for loop with more than just the number sequences generated by range().
- Replacing range() with a string will iterate through the string's characters.

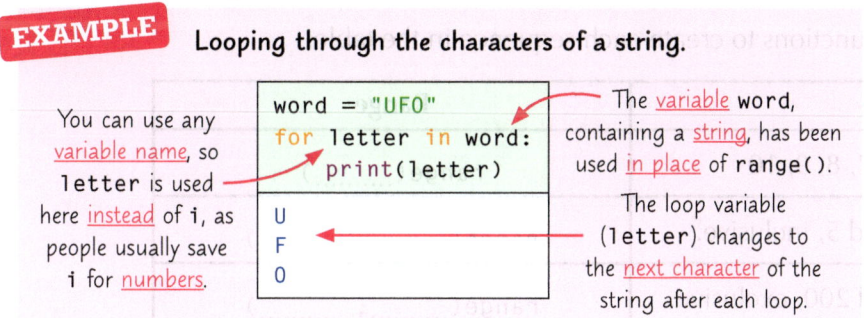

EXAMPLE Looping through the characters of a string.

You can use any variable name, so letter is used here instead of i, as people usually save i for numbers.

```
word = "UFO"
for letter in word:
    print(letter)
```
```
U
F
O
```

The variable word, containing a string, has been used in place of range().

The loop variable (letter) changes to the next character of the string after each loop.

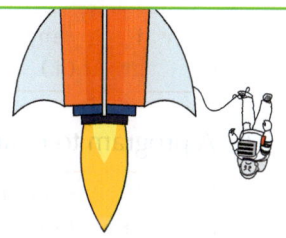

Q5 Complete the program to produce the output shown.

```
word = "Frog"
for letter in ................:
    print(................)
```
```
F
r
o
g
```

for biscuit in pack: eat(biscuit)

In case you were wondering, the 'in' bit of the for loop is always needed — you'll get a syntax error without it. You can iterate through lots of things, including lists, which you'll see in Section 7.

Section Five — Iteration

Practice Questions

Warm-Up

Q1 True or false? `range(3)` generates the number sequence: 1, 2, 3.

Q2 What numbers are in a list if it contains 'the integers 1 to 5 exclusive'?

Q3 True or false? The correct output is shown for the program on the right. →

```
for c in "Output":
    print(c)
```
```
O u t p u t
```

Practice Questions

Q1 The `range` function can accept either one, two or three numbers.

   a) What does adding a second number in `range()` allow you to do?

   ....

   ....

   b) What does the third number in `range()` represent?

   ....

Q2 The following code snippets each contain an error. Circle the error and explain why it occurs.

   a) A program to count up from 0 to 9:

   ```
   for i in range 10:
       print(i)
   ```
   ....
   ....

   b) A program to count down from 9 to 1:

   ```
   for i in range(0, 9, -1):
       print(i)
   ```
   ....
   ....

Q3 Complete the program on the right below so that it produces the same output as the program on the left.

```
word = "Guitar"
for letter in word:
    print(letter)
```
```
word = "Guitar"
for ......... in range(............(word)):
    print(............[.......])
```

Q4 Fill in the gaps in the range functions to create each sequence in the table.

Sequence	Range
0, 1, 2, 3, 4, 5, 6, 7, 8, 9, 10	range(..........)
Integers between −5 and 5, inclusive.	range(.........., ...)
Integers between 100 and 200, exclusive.	range(.........., ...)
Integers from 100 to 10, inclusive.	range(.........., ..., ...)
Odd integers between 2 and 10, descending.	range(.........., ..., ...)
The first 12 numbers in the 9 times table.	range(.........., ..., ...)

Section Five — Iteration

Coding Challenges for Section Five

You're building a reputation for your repetition, so test your chops against these coding challenges. Have a good go, then visit the link on the contents page to get example programs for each challenge.

Challenge 1 — Example

Create a program to print **multiples** of a particular **number**.
- The number should be entered by the user.
- The program should print all the multiples up to and including 100.

> The multiples of a number are just the numbers in its times table.

SOLUTION

Plan: use a `for` loop with the `range` function to generate the sequence of multiples.

① Getting a number from the user should be no sweat at this point — just make sure it's an integer.

② Using `multiple` instead of `i` isn't needed, but makes the code easier to follow.

```
number = int(input("Enter a number: "))

for multiple in range(number, 101, number):
    print(multiple)
```

```
Enter a number: 30
30
60
90
```

③ Use the number itself as the start value (any number is a multiple of itself).

④ Use 101 as the stop value, so all multiples up to 100 are included.

⑤ A quick way to go from one multiple to the next is to count in steps of the number itself, so use it as the step value.

Challenge 2

Write a program that performs a countdown for a fireworks display.

Your program should:
- Ask the user what number the countdown should start at.
- Count down the numbers, printing each one as it goes.
- After counting 1, print out "Launch the display!".

> **GOING FURTHER** — Have a go at creating a real timer by inserting the following line at the very start of your program: `import time`
> You can then use the `time.sleep(1)` command to make your program wait a real second at the end of each loop.

Challenge 3

You have been asked to create a program to control the message displayed on a shop's LED display sign.

Your program should:
- Ask the store owner to enter a message.
- Display the message by revealing one letter at a time, with each letter in uppercase (as the example shows).

```
Enter message: Open!
O
OP
OPE
OPEN
OPEN!
```

> Hint: make a new variable for the string you're printing that starts off as "" (empty).

Challenge 4

An English teacher has asked for a program they can use to test their pupils' vocabularies. Example output is shown on the right.

```
I'm thinking of a 4 letter word.
Letter 1 is s
Letter 3 is i
What is the word? slim
Correct!
```

Your program should:
- Store a secret word that the teacher can assign.
- Tell the pupil how long the word is.
- Tell the pupil every alternate letter, starting from the first.
- Ask the pupil to guess the word.
- Display a messaging saying if they're right or wrong.

> Hint: you can use string indexing (p.21) to pick out the alternate letters.

Section Five — Iteration

/ Section Six — More Iteration

More Iteration

Learning Objectives

for loops are useful for lots of things, but they do have their limits. Fortunately for you, there is another kind of iteration — continue reading to find out more.

- Learn the meaning of count-controlled and condition-controlled iteration.
- Understand how for loops are count-controlled iteration.
- Be able to visualise condition-controlled loops in flowcharts.

for loops are count-controlled

1) for loops are nice when you know how many times you want something to repeat.

```
for count in range(6):
    print("Welcome to Section Six")
```
 This repeats 6 times.

KEY TERMS: Count-controlled loops (or **definite loops**) repeat a set number of times.

2) This is an example of a count-controlled loop — when the loop ends is controlled by a counter reaching a certain value.
3) But sometimes you don't know how many times code will need to repeat.
4) For example, suppose you want to repeat a question until the user enters a correct answer. They may get it correct on the first attempt, or it might take 5, 10, or even 1 million attempts — the number isn't known.
5) In situations like this you need a different kind of loop.

You can't use a for loop as you don't know what number to put in range().

```
for attempt in range(   ):
    answer = input("Enter answer: ")
```
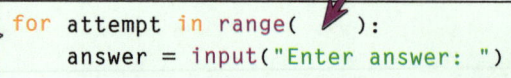

Iteration can have no limits

KEY TERMS: Condition-controlled loops (or **indefinite loops**) repeat code based on whether a condition is True or not.

- A condition-controlled loop repeats code based on a condition.
- In Python, when this kind of loop ends is controlled by a condition becoming False. Code repeats while the condition is True — there's no limit to how many times.
- Before seeing how this can be done in your programs (see the next page), take a look at how this is represented in a flowchart.

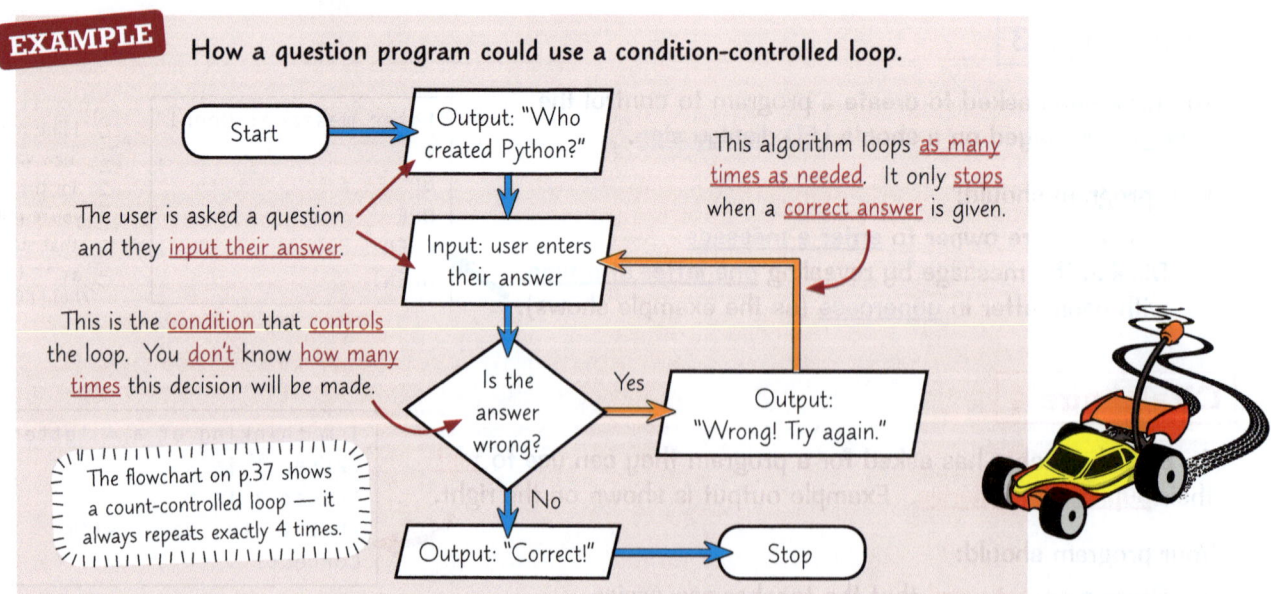

How a question program could use a condition-controlled loop.

I've saved my very best iteration joke just for you: look down...

Many real-life programs use a mix of these two kinds of loops, so it's important to get used to both. Now without further ado, let's see how you go about coding condition-controlled loops in Python.

look up...

while Loops

Learning Objectives

It should come as no surprise that Python can do condition-controlled iteration — I mean, that previous page just came right out and said it, no subtlety whatsoever.
- Learn the structure and syntax of a while loop.
- Understand how while loops are condition-controlled iteration.
- Understand how an infinite loop can occur and how to prevent it.
- Be able to use Boolean operators in while loop conditions.

while loops are condition-controlled

Remember, != means 'not equal to' (p.26).

1) Python has a condition-controlled loop called a while loop.
2) Instead of repeating code a set number of times (like for), it repeats until a condition is broken.

EXAMPLE Using a while loop to program the flowchart on the previous page.

A while loop begins with a condition followed by a colon.

Any indented code is inside the while loop. It runs repeatedly until the loop ends.

This code is outside the loop (as it isn't indented). It only runs after the loop ends.

If a correct answer is given first, the indented code never runs.

```
answer = input("Who created Python? ")

while answer != "Guido van Rossum":
    print("Wrong! Try again.")
    answer = input("Who created Python? ")

print("Correct!")
```

```
Who created Python? CGP
Wrong! Try again.
Who created Python? Rossum van Guido
Wrong! Try again.
Who created Python? Guido van Rossum
Correct!
```

This condition is checked. If it's True, then the indented code runs, otherwise the loop ends.

The user is asked to change their answer. After this, the program goes back up to the condition and checks it again.

Q1 How does this program behave if "guido van rossum" is input as the answer?

The condition needs to eventually become False

- Be careful — if your while loop condition is never False (so always True) then your program will get stuck in an infinite loop.
- This often happens if you forget to change a variable that a condition is based on.

COMMON PROBLEMS Accidently creating an infinite loop (or 'How to annoy the user').

The user is asked once to enter the password.

Only the indented code inside the loop is repeated, so password is never changed after it's first set (a logic error).

A wrong password means the loop condition will never be False, so the same line is printed again and again, forever...*

```
password = input("Enter your password: ")

while password != "password123":
    print("Wrong! Try again.")

print("Password is correct.")
```

```
Enter your password: 123
Wrong! Try again.
Wrong! Try again.
Wrong! Try again.
```

!= is used, so that if the user gets the password wrong, the loop condition will be True.

*If you get stuck in an infinite loop, don't panic. In the IDLE Shell, you can click "Interrupt Execution" in the Shell menu (or use the given keyboard shortcut).

Section Six — More Iteration

while Loops

Use Boolean operators to check multiple conditions

1) What condition goes between 'while' and ':' is entirely up to you. Any bit of Python that results in either True or False can be used.
2) This means you can use Boolean operators to make more complex conditions.

See p.27 for a refresher on the Boolean operators.

EXAMPLE The 'BuyYourFruitsElsewhere' cornershop refuses to sell fruit for less than £10. The following code is part of their item pricing program.

An employee enters an item's category and price.

A while loop is used to ask for new input if it detects fruit being priced too cheaply.

```
category = input("Enter category: ")
price = float(input("Enter price: £"))

while category == "fruit" and price < 10:
    print("That's far too cheap!")
    category = input("Enter category: ")
    price = float(input("Enter price: £"))

print("That's allowed.")
```

and is used to check the two conditions. This means the loop runs if both of the conditions are True at the same time, and ends when either becomes False.

Here both conditions are True, so the while loop runs the indented code.

Now the price condition is False, so the while loop ends.

```
Enter category: fruit
Enter price: £1.50
That's far too cheap!
Enter category: fruit
Enter price: £14.99
That's allowed.
```

```
Enter category: crisps
Enter price: £1.75
That's allowed.
```

Here the category condition is False, so the indented code never runs.

Q2 What happens in this program if the user inputs the price of crisps at £14.99?

3) You can make conditions based on all sorts of things that you've seen earlier in this book.

EXAMPLE Using the len function (p.20) to validate the length of user input.

The condition checks the different ways the user's input could be invalid. There could be too few or too many letters — len() is used to count how many there are.

```
word = input("Enter a word with 3 to 6 letters: ")

while len(word) < 3 or len(word) > 6:
    word = input("Try again please: ")

print("Was that so hard?")
```

or is used to join the two parts of the condition, because the input is invalid if either part is True.

```
Enter a word with 3 to 6 letters: um
Try again please: spaghetti
Try again please: help
Was that so hard?
```

Here the first part of the condition is True, so the loop runs.

The second part of the condition is now True, so the loop runs again.

Both parts of the condition are False, so the loop ends.

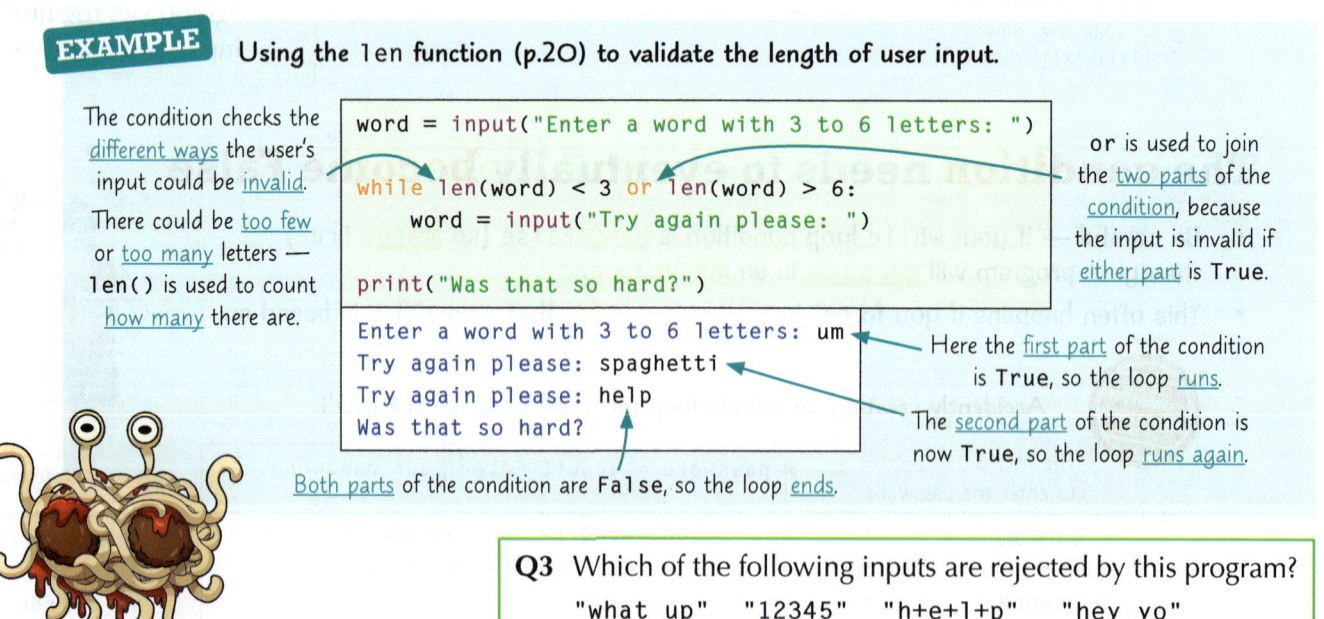

Q3 Which of the following inputs are rejected by this program?
"what up"   "12345"   "h+e+l+p"   "hey yo"

Repeat after me: "I must not sleep while programming, I...Zzzz"
Be careful with the operators you use — it's easy to make a condition opposite to what you want. The key thing to remember is that while loops continue until the condition is broken (i.e. False).

Section Six — More Iteration

Nesting Statements

Learning Objectives: Sometimes you want to make a decision inside a loop, or iterate inside a selection, or whatever wild idea you might come up with. This reckless behaviour is called nesting.
- Understand what nesting is in programming.
- Be able to write programs with nested statements.

Statements can be nested inside each other

Nesting is when one block of code is put inside another block of code.

EXAMPLE Nested if statements can make more complicated programs.

```
hearJoke = input("Do you want to hear a joke? ")
if hearJoke == "yes":
    answer = input("Why did the python cross the road? ")
    if answer == "To get to the other ssside.":
        print("Oh, so you've heard this before :(")
    else:
        print("To get to the other ssside. Hahaha.")
print("Goodbye.")
```

Everything indented to this line is inside the first if statement — this includes the second if statement.

The else clause belongs to the second if statement, because the indentation matches.

If the user doesn't answer "Yes" to the first question, the program skips to the end.

The second if statement should be skipped if the user doesn't want to hear the joke — that's why it's nested inside the first.

```
Do you want to hear a joke? Yes
Why did the python cross the road? Dunno
To get to the other ssside. Hahaha.
Goodbye.
```

```
Do you want to hear a joke? No
Goodbye.
```

Q1 How could you modify this program to show a suitable message if the user answers something other than "yes" to the first question?

Nesting works with iteration too

EXAMPLE Checking if a user has entered a valid binary number.

```
number = input("Enter a binary number: ")
isValid = True
for digit in number:
    if digit != "0" and digit != "1":
        isValid = False

if isValid == True:
    print("That's binary alright.")
else:
    print("0s and 1s only, please...")
```

The input is assumed to be valid before it is checked.

The if statement is nested inside the for loop, so that every time the loop repeats, the if condition is checked again for the next digit.

Nesting works with while loops too.

If you're not familiar, binary numbers are made up of just 0s and 1s — computers use them to process data.

The for loop goes through each digit, one at a time.

If any digit is not a 0 or a 1 then the input is invalid.

```
Enter a binary number: 102
0s and 1s only, please...
```

2 isn't a binary digit, so isValid ends up False.

Nesting Nesting Nesting Nesting is cool is cool is cool is cool...

The key to nesting in Python is making sure the indentation is correct. Each level of nesting needs another tab and the right bits need to line up — you'll learn to spot bad indentation with practice.

Section Six — More Iteration

Practice Questions

Warm-Up

Q1 What kind of loop is a `while` loop — count-controlled or condition-controlled?

Q2 How can you stop a program running if it gets into an infinite loop?

Q3 True or false? An `if` statement can be nested inside a `while` loop.

Practice Questions

Q1 Raf has written the cheerleader program on the right. Fill in the gap so that the program continues to cheer as long as Raf types "yes".

```
cheer = "yes"
while ............ ............ ............ :
    print("Come on Raf!")
    cheer = input("Continue? ")
```

Q2 Write the output of the program below if the user enters the numbers 10, 25, then 35 when asked.

```
num = int(input("Enter a number: "))

while num <= 25:
    print(num - 5)
    num = int(input("Enter a number: "))

print("Bye")
```

Q3 The program below is meant to make sure a user enters a name that is longer than 3 characters but shorter than 15 characters.

```
name = input("Input a name: ")

while len(name) > 3 and len(name) < 15:
    print("Invalid name. Try again.")
    input("Input a name: ")

print("Success")
```

a) Describe two errors in this program.

1. ....
   ....

2. ....
   ....

b) Rewrite the program, in the box above, to correct the errors.

Q4 Complete the program on the right so that it prints "Bad" for each letter that isn't lowercase and "Good" for each letter that is lowercase.

```
word = input("Enter a word in lowercase: ")
for letter in word:
```

Hint: you'll need to use the .lower() function here — see p.20 for a reminder.

Section Six — More Iteration

Coding Challenges for Section Six

Oh, hello again — it's been a while since I've seen you in these parts. You know the drill by now — have at these Coding Challenges, then visit the link on the contents page to get example programs for each challenge.

Challenge 1 — Example

Write a program that asks a user for their first name and their last name.
To make sure the user actually types these in, check both of their names are at least 2 characters long. Keep asking for these until they are.

SOLUTION

Plan: use while loops to ask the user to reenter each name until they're both long enough.

① Ask for each name separately, as both need to be checked. It makes sense to start with the first name.

② Ask the user to reenter their name if it's too short. Remember to reassign the variable, so the loop doesn't repeat endlessly.

③ You can use the same code for the last name, just change the message and variable.

④ If you'd like, you can end with a personalised message.

```
firstName = input("What's your first name? ")
while len(firstName) < 2:
    firstName = input("Too short, try again: ")

lastName = input("What's your last name? ")
while len(lastName) < 2:
    lastName = input("Too short, try again: ")

print("Thank you,", firstName, lastName)
```

Challenge 2

Jeanne Calment is officially the oldest person that has ever lived — she lived to be 122 years old. Write a program to check whether someone has broken this world record.

Your program should:
- Ask the user to enter their age (don't forget to make it an integer).
- Reject their input until an age in the range 0 to 130 (exclusive) is given.
- After the input is accepted, if the age is above Jeanne's age say "Wow, that's a world record!", otherwise say "Keep going, no world record yet.".

'exclusive' here means 0 and 130 need to be rejected, but all numbers in between are fine.

Challenge 3

A company makes burglar alarms that can be disabled with a code. Each alarm is preset with a master code, and the user can set their own personal code which disables it too.

The company wants you to write a test program for their alarms.
Your program should:
- Store a master code (e.g. 19970804).
- Ask the user to input their personal code (e.g. 1875).
- Tell the user the alarm will now be tested, and repeat a message saying the alarm is going off until a correct code has been entered.
- Once a correct code has been entered, say that the alarm is disabled.

Challenge 4

Write a program that allows a user to set a new password.
A password should be accepted only if it has the following features:
- It doesn't match their old password (store this in your program).
- It is not entirely lowercase and not entirely uppercase.
- It has length between 8 and 16 characters (inclusive).

If an invalid password is entered, tell the user what was wrong and have them try again until one is accepted.

Video Solution

Section Six — More Iteration

Section Seven — Lists

Lists

Learning Objectives

I've made a top-ten list of Python's best functions — you won't believe what's at number one... Before I reveal it, you better learn about how Python handles lists.

- Learn what data structures are and why they are useful.
- Be able to create a list and use indexes to access items.

Data structures group data together

1) So far you've only used variables to keep hold of single pieces of data.
2) This is a messy problem when you have lots of similar items that result in lots of similar variables that you need to keep track of.
3) In situations like this, you'd benefit from using a data structure to group the items together, then:
   - You only have one variable to name and keep track of.
   - Everything is more organised as the data is kept together.
   - You can use lots of handy functions (see the next page).

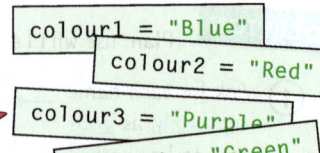

KEY TERMS: A data structure is an organised collection of items stored under one name.

GOING FURTHER: There are lots of other data structures that you'll learn at GCSE and beyond, such as tuples, dictionaries and sets.

Lists hold multiple items

- A list in Python is exactly what it sounds like — a simple list of data values.
- A list can contain a mix of different data types (strings, integers, floats, etc.).

EXAMPLE Creating a list and checking its length.

```
colours = ["Blue", "Red", "Purple", "Green"]
print("The list is:", colours)
print("It has", len(colours), "items.")

The list is: ['Blue', 'Red', 'Purple', 'Green']
It has 4 items.
```

Use square brackets, [ ], to make a list. Put the items inside and separate them with commas (the spacing is optional).

Printing a list simply shows the whole thing to the user.

Use len() to find the length of a list (i.e. how many items are in it).

You can make an empty list by using an empty set of brackets, e.g. colours = [ ]. It has nothing it in, so its length is 0. You can then add items using the functions on the next page.

Use indexes to pick out items

To get one particular item in a list, you use its index — just like with string characters back on p.21.

```
print("First item:", colours[0])
First item: Blue
```

The first item of a list has index 0 (the colours list from the example above is used here).

Q1 What are the two possible indexes of the colour "Red"?

```
print("Last item:", colours[3])
Last item: Green
```

```
print("Last item:", colours[-1])
Last item: Green
```

The index of the last item is one less than the list's length... ...or you can use a negative index.

Negative indexes start from the end at −1, then go to −2, −3, etc, just like with strings.

So, my fav' Python function? It's topTenFunctions[0] of course...

List names follow the same variable naming rules that you saw on page 13. Any data type can go in a list, even other data structures too — you can have lists inside of lists, as you'll see later.

Working with Lists

Learning Objectives

Imagine doing a food shop with a list that never changes. Not great, unless you don't mind the same dinners every week for eternity — and no judgement here if so...

- Be able to change an item in a list using its index.
- Be able to add items to the list using `.append()` or `.insert()`.
- Be able to remove items from a list using `.remove()`.

Use indexes to change items

You saw on the previous page how to pick out an item using its index. As long as an item already exists at an index, you can change it too.

A list of sports is created here, but the data contains a typo.

The second item, at index position 1, is changed here, correcting the mistake.

```
sports = ["Netball", "Flatball", "Rugby"]
print("Before:", sports)
sports[1] = "Football"
print("After:", sports)

Before: ['Netball', 'Flatball', 'Rugby']
After: ['Netball', 'Football', 'Rugby']
```

Q1 Write a line of code that would change the item "Rugby" to "Golf" in this list.

Three list functions to help you out

You were promised data structures come with 'handy functions' — well, here you go...

EXAMPLE Use `.append()` to add to the end of a list.

`.append()` is typed after the list's name, sports, with the new item inside the brackets.

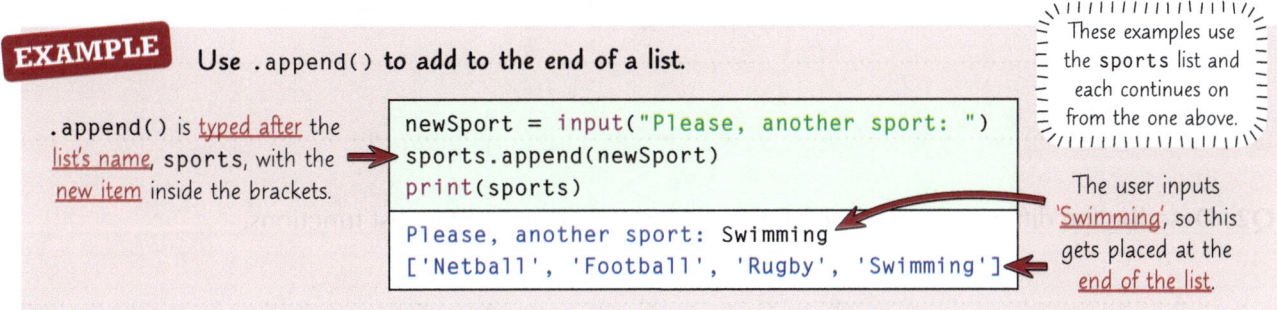

These examples use the sports list and each continues on from the one above.

The user inputs 'Swimming', so this gets placed at the end of the list.

```
newSport = input("Please, another sport: ")
sports.append(newSport)
print(sports)

Please, another sport: Swimming
['Netball', 'Football', 'Rugby', 'Swimming']
```

EXAMPLE Use `.insert()` to put an item at a particular index position.

`.insert()` needs two things inside its brackets: the index position (where you want the item to go) and the item itself.

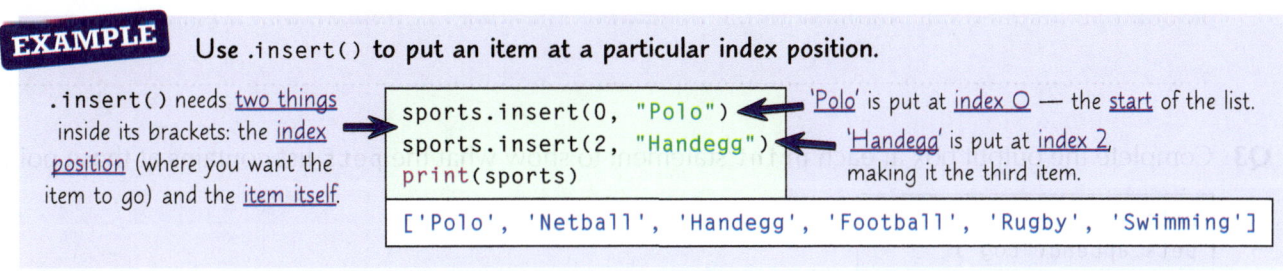

'Polo' is put at index 0 — the start of the list.

'Handegg' is put at index 2, making it the third item.

```
sports.insert(0, "Polo")
sports.insert(2, "Handegg")
print(sports)

['Polo', 'Netball', 'Handegg', 'Football', 'Rugby', 'Swimming']
```

EXAMPLE Use `.remove()` to delete an item from a list.

If the same item appears more than once in a list, `.remove()` only deletes the first one that it finds.

`.remove()` only needs to know the item you want gone — that goes in the brackets.

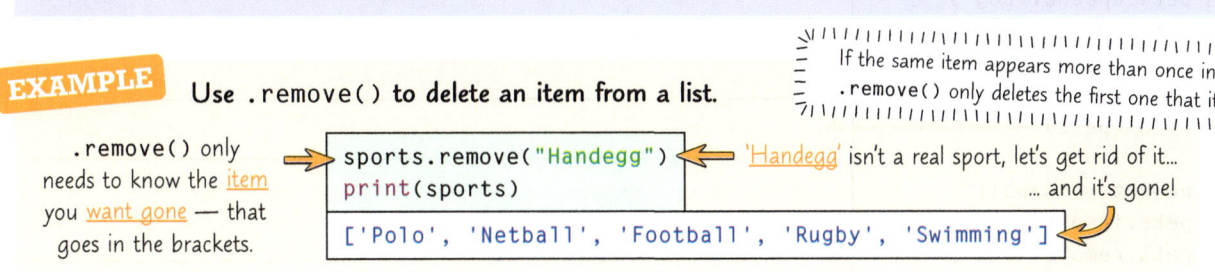

'Handegg' isn't a real sport, let's get rid of it...

... and it's gone!

```
sports.remove("Handegg")
print(sports)

['Polo', 'Netball', 'Football', 'Rugby', 'Swimming']
```

Done — you can now .remove(this page) from your to-do list...

Python kicks up a fuss if you use an index where no item exists. For instance, if you use `sports[99]` in the above example, you'll get an `IndexError` as there's nowhere near 100 items.

Section Seven — Lists

Practice Questions

Warm-Up

Q1 What is a data structure?

Q2 True or false? The first item in a list has an index of 1.

Q3 What is wrong with the code in this box? →
```
numbers = [5, 6, 7]
print(numbers(2))
```

Practice Questions

Q1 The line of code below creates a list of words.
```
words = ["love", "pants", "alligator", "hate", "socks", "caiman"]
```

a) What data type are the items in this list? ....

b) Complete the output for the following lines of code.

　i) `print(len(words))`

　ii) `print(words[-3])`

c) Write a line of code to output "I love to put socks on my alligator".
   Three words must be taken from the `words` list using indexes.

d) Explain the error caused by this line of code. → `words.remove("crocodile")`

   ....

   ....

Q2 Describe the different purposes of the `.append()` and `.insert()` list functions.

   ....

   ....

   ....

Q3 Complete the output box at each `print` statement to show what the `pets` list contains at those points.

```
pets = []
pets.append("Dog")
pets.append("Cat")
pets.append("Snake")
pets[0] = "Fish"
print(pets)

newPet = "Rabbit"
pets.insert(1, "Budgie")
pets.remove("Cat")
print(pets)

pets.append(newPet)
pets[-2] = "Ferret"
print(pets)
```

Section Seven — Lists

Iterating through Lists

Learning Objectives

Here's how to combine two really important concepts: for loops and lists. Doing so opens up a lot of potential in your programs.

- Be able to use a for loop to iterate through the items of a list.
- Be able to iterate through a list using a for loop with range().

for loops go through items one by one

1) Lists can get quite big in real-life programs — sometimes they'll contain thousands or even millions of items.
2) Manually accessing thousands of items one by one using their indexes would take forever, and your program would be wrong if the list ever changed length.
3) for loops can solve this problem in a couple of ways.

```
print(naughtyList[0])
print(naughtyList[1])
```
A long time later...
```
print(naughtyList[100000])
print(naughtyList[100001])
```

EXAMPLE Here's the simplest way to loop through items in a list.

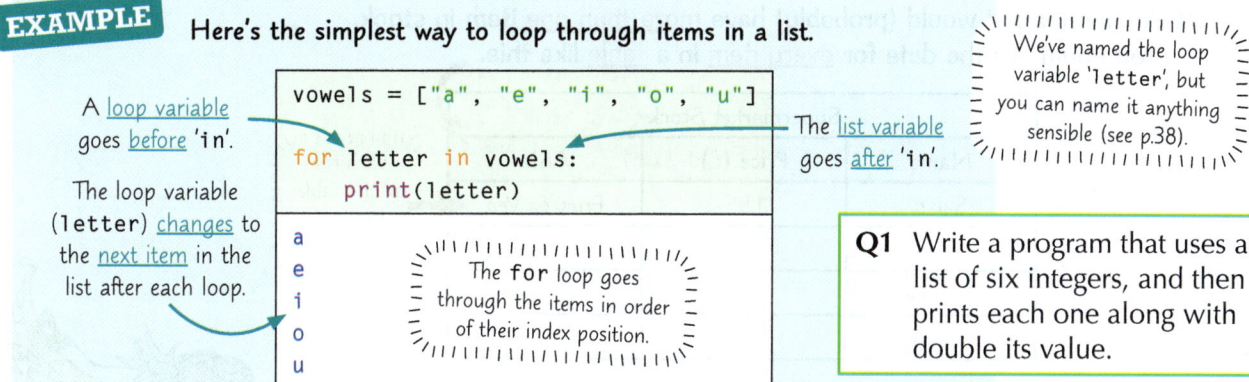

```
vowels = ["a", "e", "i", "o", "u"]

for letter in vowels:
    print(letter)
```

A loop variable goes before 'in'.

The list variable goes after 'in'.

The loop variable (letter) changes to the next item in the list after each loop.

```
a
e
i
o
u
```

The for loop goes through the items in order of their index position.

We've named the loop variable 'letter', but you can name it anything sensible (see p.38).

Q1 Write a program that uses a list of six integers, and then prints each one along with double its value.

Use range() if you want to use the index too

- When looping through a list, you sometimes need to know the index of each item, as well as the items themselves.
- The trick to making this happen is to loop through the indexes instead of the items.

Look back at p.40 for how to generate numbers with range().

EXAMPLE Showing the items in a list next to their position.

```
vowels = ["a", "e", "i", "o", "u"]

for i in range(len(vowels)):
    print("Vowel", i+1, "is", vowels[i])
```

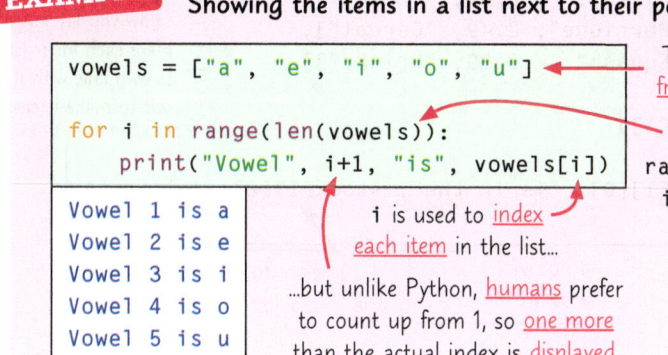

```
Vowel 1 is a
Vowel 2 is e
Vowel 3 is i
Vowel 4 is o
Vowel 5 is u
```

The items in this list are indexed from 0 (for "a") up to 4 (for "u").

Stick the length of the list in range(), so that the loop variable i covers all the possible indexes.

i is used to index each item in the list...

...but unlike Python, humans prefer to count up from 1, so one more than the actual index is displayed.

You could use range(5) here, but using len() to find the length is better in general as you won't always know what the length is.

COMMON PROBLEMS

A common mistake is to mix up the two examples shown on this page. You can't do something like this:
```
for i in vowels:
    print(vowels[i])
```
Try this code and see what error you get.

What kind of list has the best sense of fashion? A stylist...

The first example above is much simpler and easier to read, so it's the one to use if you don't need the index numbers. The best way to know if that's the case is to plan out your algorithms first.

Section Seven — Lists

2D Lists

Learning Objectives

What if you want to put a list inside a list? Well, you absolutely can, as this page will show. Be sure you're good with regular lists first, as 2D lists are kinda tricky.

- Know the difference between a 1D and a 2D list.
- Understand how a 2D list can represent data in a table.
- Be able to create a 2D list and use indexes to get items.

Lists can have other lists as items

1) The lists you've seen so far have all been one-dimensional (1D) — meaning they contain only simple items like strings and integers.
2) E.g. this list contains the name, price and aisle of one item at a supermarket.

   ```
   item = ["Salad", 1.55, "Fruit & Veg"]
   ```

3) A supermarket would (probably) have more than one item in stock. You could put the data for every item in a table like this.

Supermarket Stock		
Name	Price (£)	Aisle
Salad	1.55	Fruit & Veg
Pizza	2.99	Frozen
Porridge	2.49	Cereal
Squash	1.29	Drinks

   Each row of this table represents a 1D list.

4) Imagine making a list for every row and then making one giant list that has all these smaller lists as its items.
5) A list of lists like this, that represents the whole table, is called a two-dimensional (2D) list.

EXAMPLE Using a 2D list to store the names, prices and aisles of food in a supermarket.

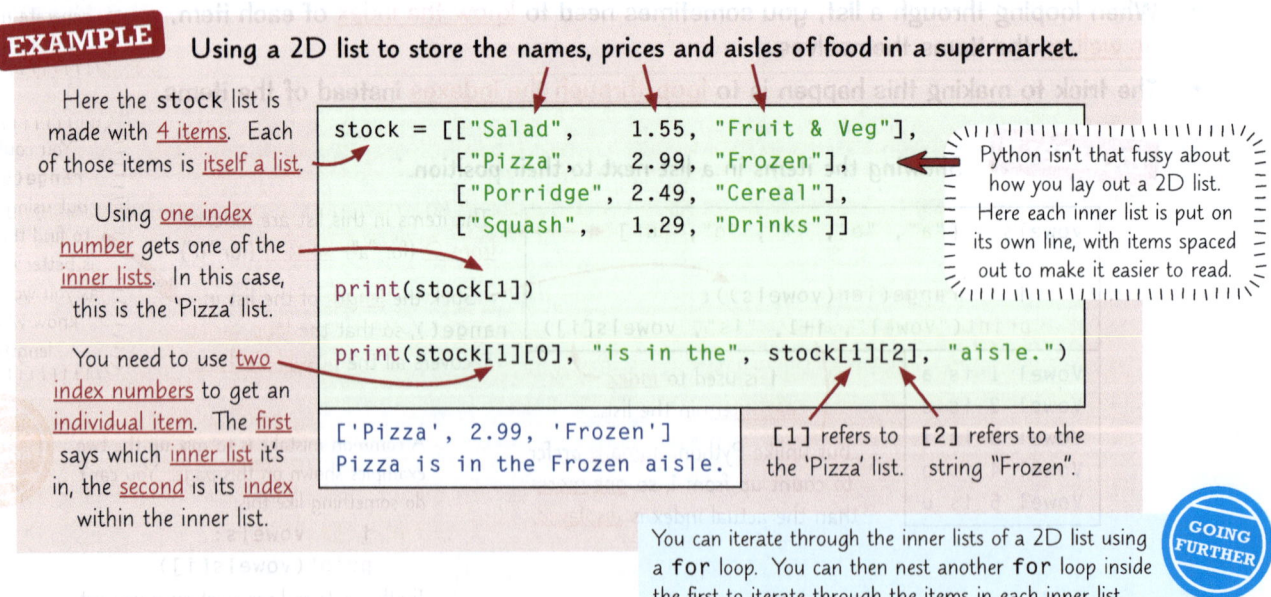

Here the stock list is made with 4 items. Each of those items is itself a list.

Using one index number gets one of the inner lists. In this case, this is the 'Pizza' list.

You need to use two index numbers to get an individual item. The first says which inner list it's in, the second is its index within the inner list.

```
stock = [["Salad",   1.55, "Fruit & Veg"],
         ["Pizza",   2.99, "Frozen"],
         ["Porridge", 2.49, "Cereal"],
         ["Squash",  1.29, "Drinks"]]

print(stock[1])

print(stock[1][0], "is in the", stock[1][2], "aisle.")
```

```
['Pizza', 2.99, 'Frozen']
Pizza is in the Frozen aisle.
```

Python isn't that fussy about how you lay out a 2D list. Here each inner list is put on its own line, with items spaced out to make it easier to read.

[1] refers to the 'Pizza' list.   [2] refers to the string "Frozen".

You can iterate through the inner lists of a 2D list using a `for` loop. You can then nest another `for` loop inside the first to iterate through the items in each inner list.

GOING FURTHER

Code pun time: `["D", "D"]`. Get it? Okay, I'll see myself out...

2D lists can be tricky to get your head around at first, so if you're able to make a 2D list and are able to use a correct pair of indexes to get a particular item from it, then that's a perfect start.

Section Seven — Lists

Practice Questions

Warm-Up

Q1 True or false? The index of the last element in a list is equal to the length of the list.

Q2 In terms of indexes, in what order does this loop go through the items? ➡ `for page in contents`

Q3 Which of the following is a correct way to access an item of a 2D list?

`myList(0)(0)`   `myList[0][0]`   `myList[0, 0]`   `myList[0:0]`

Practice Questions

Q1 The code below should print only the words shorter than 4 characters.

a) Fill in the gaps to complete the program.

```
noises = ["Moo", "Neigh", "Ribbit", "Oink", "Baa"]
for ........ in range(len(........................)):
    if len(............................) < 4:
        print(............................)
```

b) Rewrite the program to use a `for` loop without `range()`.

```
noises = ["Moo", "Neigh", "Ribbit", "Oink", "Baa"]
```

Q2 A 2D list is created below.

```
groups = [["Jess", "AJ",    "Benny"],
          ["Igor", "Tobi",  "Eve"],
          ["Amna", "Luiza", "Zaynab"]]
```

Complete the table so that the code on the left produces the output on the right.

Code	Output
`print(groups[0][1])`	
	Jess
`print(groups[1])`	
	Tobi
	Luiza

Q3 The code on the right is meant to print each number in the list. It outputs three numbers before an error occurs. What is wrong?

```
values = [4, 1, 0, 5, 3]
for i in values:
    print(values[i])
```

```
3
1
4
IndexError: list index
out of range
```

....

....

....

....

Coding Challenges for Section Seven

The page has changed colour again — that can only mean one thing... Another round of Coding Challenges! Try your darndest, then visit the link on the contents page to get example programs for each challenge.

Challenge 1 — Example

Write a program that lets a user enter a word, then searches through a list of file names to find any that contain the given word.

Hint: the .count() function seen on p.20 will come in handy here.

SOLUTION

Plan: loop through the list of file names and test each to see if they contain the user's word at least once.

① A list with a few items is created for testing.

② A for loop is used to go through the file names. This form is suitable as the indexes won't be needed.

```
files = ["helloword.py", "homework.txt", "wordsearch.jpg", "test.html"]
word = input("Enter a word to search for: ")
for filename in files:
    if filename.count(word) > 0:
        print("Potential match:", filename)
```

③ .count() tells you how many times the word appears in each filename.

```
Enter a word to search for: word
Potential match: helloword.py
Potential match: wordsearch.jpg
```

④ A count greater than 0 means the word was found at least once.

Challenge 2

You've been asked to write a program to track the teams in an esports competition.

Your program should:
- Ask the user to enter 4 team names, one at a time, and add each to a list.
- Then ask the user which team to eliminate and remove this team from the list.
- Keep going until only 1 team is left, then declare that team as the winner.

Challenge 3

Heather wants to know the average length of her guinea pigs. Write a program to help her out.

To calculate the average length your program needs to:
- Calculate a total by adding up all the lengths.
- Divide the total by the number of guinea pigs.

```
lengths = [22.5, 33.0, 24.6, 29.8, 31.1]
```

Your program should work with any list of lengths, but you can test it using the one above.

These are all in cm.

Challenge 4

A school system has a list of pupils' first names and a list of their surnames.

```
firstNames = ["Kelly", "Manok", "Akash", "Tatiana", "Nicolas", "Simran"]
surnames = ["Jones", "Olsen", "Khan", "Roberts", "Clark", "Kumar"]
```

These lists are ordered so that matching parts of a pupil's full name have the same index position.

It would be more convenient to store both parts of each name together. Write a program that creates a single 2D list that stores the first name and surname of each pupil together.

Your program should:
- Start by creating an empty list called pupils.
- For each pupil in the original lists:
  - Create a new list containing their first name and surname, e.g. ["Kelly", "Jones"].
  - Append this new list to pupils.
- Print the entire pupils list once it's done, so you can check you've got it correct.

Section Eight — Subroutines

Built-in Subroutines

Learning Objectives

Subroutines eh? Yep, you've been using them all along. One was even snuck into the 'Hello, world!' program, all the way back in Section One. It's time to learn what they are.

- Learn what a subroutine is.
- Understand the purpose of subroutines.
- Learn about built-in subroutines and why they're useful.

Subroutines are reusable blocks of code

1) A subroutine is a block of code that has been given a name.
2) They're like a mini-program — usually performing one particular task.
3) You only need to write the code once, then a subroutine can be used many times within the same program and reused in other programs too.

Subroutines are sometimes called 'sub programs'.

Built-in subroutines are ready to use

- A built-in subroutine is one that comes included with Python.
- You can use them in your own programs straight away.
- You've seen lots of them in this book already — here's just a few:

```
print()      int()        range()
 p.10                       p.40-41
input()      .upper()     .remove()
 p.11         p.20          p.51
```

GOING FURTHER

In Python, the subroutines with no full stop are a type of subroutine called a function and the ones with a full stop are another type called a method. Things like strings and lists have lots more built-in methods you could use.

- They all work in different ways, but the round brackets after the name are a dead giveaway that they're subroutines.

Built-in subroutines are tried and tested

1) Some built-in subroutines are included with Python as they'd be hard to code yourself.
2) Others do quite simple jobs but using them saves you time and effort.
3) They've all been well-tested, so they're unlikely to contain errors.

sum() adds up a list

EXAMPLE Using the built-in subroutine sum() versus coding it yourself.

The sum subroutine adds up all of the numbers in a list and gives you the result.

```
values = [5, 10, 25, 2, 9]

total = sum(values)

print("The total is", total)

The total is 51
```

5 + 10 + 25 + 2 + 9 = 51

This isn't that hard to code yourself, but it's more work.

```
values = [5, 10, 25, 2, 9]

total = 0
for number in values:
    total = total + number

print("The total is", total)

The total is 51
```

Instead of using sum(), you could loop through the list and add each number to a running total.

Built-in Subroutines

sorted() puts lists in order

1) Writing a program to sort a list of values is a tough job — it's the kind of program you might make for yourself during a GCSE course.
2) Happily, Python has the built-in subroutine sorted() that you can use right now.

EXAMPLE Using the built-in subroutine sorted() to put a list in order.

The letters in this list are in no particular order.

sorted() gives you an ordered copy of the list.

The original unordered list isn't changed.

```
unordered = ["d", "a", "e", "c", "b"]
ordered = sorted(unordered)
print("Unordered:", unordered)
print("Ordered:", ordered)

Unordered: ['d', 'a', 'e', 'c', 'b']
Ordered: ['a', 'b', 'c', 'd', 'e']
```

The unordered list is put inside the brackets.

sorted() puts a list of strings in alphabetical order.

Q1 sorted() works on lists of numbers too.
a) Write a program that uses sorted() to sort an unordered list of numbers.
b) Are the numbers sorted in ascending or descending order?
c) What error do you get if you try to sort a list containing a mix of strings and numbers?

Modules are full of useful subroutines

1) A module is a collection of subroutines you can add to your program.
2) Some modules come with Python and some are made by other people.
3) The random module is a fun one — it lets you write a program that does random things, so that it behaves differently each time it's run.

GOING FURTHER There are some other modules that come pre-installed with Python, like math, time and turtle (see Section 9). Others have to be installed, like pygame, which is used for making games.

EXAMPLE Using randint() from the random module to pick a random integer.

To use a module, you need to first tell Python to include it with an import line. This must go at the start of your program.

randint() is one of the subroutines that's in the random module.

```
import random

print("I'm going to give you some money.")
print("Let me think...")

amount = random.randint(1, 1000)

print("I'll give you", amount, "pounds!")

I'm going to give you some money.
Let me think...
I'll give you 102 pounds!
```

randint() chooses a random integer between two values (including both as possible results).

Every time you run this program, you'll (almost certainly) get a different result.

---

sorted(["coders", "all", "subroutines", "brilliant", "reuse"])

This book covers some of the more important built-in subroutines just to get you started, but there are plenty more awaiting you. Don't forget the import line for those that are stashed in modules.

Practice Questions

Warm-Up

Q1 Describe what a subroutine is.

Q2 Which built-in subroutine tells you the number of characters in a string?

Q3 What is the result of `sum([1, 2, 3])`?

Q4 What line of code needs to be included in a program before the `random.randint` subroutine can be used?

Practice Questions

Q1 Give two benefits of using built-in subroutines like `sum` and `sorted`.

   1. ....

   ....

   2. ....

   ....

Q2 Tick whether the following statements are True or False.

Statement	True	False
This line of code contains an error: `sorted(3, 1, 2)`		
A module is a collection of subroutines you can add to a program.		
A `for` loop is a built-in subroutine.		

Q3 Complete the output of the program on the right.

```
numbers = [5, 1, -6, 3, 15, 7]
numbers.append(-2)
numbers = sorted(numbers)
numbers.append(4)
print(numbers)
```

Q4 Look at the program below.

```
words = ["turtle", "adverb", "magic", "nonsense", "flying"]
letter = input("Please enter a letter: ").lower()

total = 0
for i in range(len(words)):
    total = total + words[i].count(letter)

print("The letter was found", total, "times.")
```

a) Underline all of the built-in subroutines in this program.

b) Explain what this program does.

....

....

Section Eight — Subroutines

Defining Subroutines

Learning Objectives

Built-in subroutines are handy, but there isn't always one that does what you want. Sometimes you just need to roll up your sleeves and create your own subroutines.

- Understand the meaning of decomposition.
- Be able to define your own subroutines.
- Be able to build a program using your own subroutines.

Decomposed programs are easier to code

1) When solving a big problem, it's helpful to decompose it into smaller problems.
2) You can do this in your coding by breaking down a complex program into simpler subroutines.
3) You can use a mix of built-in subroutines, subroutines from modules that are already written, and subroutines that you write yourself.

KEY TERMS — **Decomposition** is breaking a big problem down into smaller problems.

Create your own subroutines using def

- The diagram on the right shows the decomposition of a program for a times tables quiz.
- The following examples show how to code each part and put them together to build a complete program.
- To do this, you could create your own subroutines — one for each part of the program.

Times Tables Quiz
- Ask the user their name and welcome them.
- Show the user a menu with options to choose from.
- Test the user on the times table of their choice.

EXAMPLE — Creating a subroutine to welcome the user, then calling it.

This example starts a program that's built across p.60-63.

A subroutine definition starts at def and contains the indented lines of code that follow.

```
def welcomePlayer():
    name = input("Hi! What's your name? ")
    print("Welcome to the quiz", name)

welcomePlayer()
```

```
Hi! What's your name? Mary
Welcome to the quiz Mary
```

The name of the subroutine must be followed by brackets and a colon.

The code inside a subroutine doesn't run until it's called.

To call a subroutine just write its name followed by brackets — then the code will be run.

This line is outside the subroutine — it's part of the main program.

KEY TERMS — **Calling** a subroutine is when you write its name to run its code.

- Another subroutine is needed to show the quiz menu to the user. It will simply print out a list of options they can choose from.

COMMON PROBLEMS — Three easy mistakes when defining your own subroutine.

Subroutine names must follow the same rules as variable names (p.13), so no spaces are allowed.

```
def show Menu:
    print("Select an option (1-3).")
    print("1. Play 7 times table.")
    print("2. Play 9 times table.")
    print("3. Quit.")
```

Brackets () are needed between the subroutine name and the colon.

The code after the def line should be indented.

Q1 Correct the mistakes in this code to create a working showMenu subroutine.

COMMON PROBLEMS — Be careful when naming subroutines. Make sure the name is unique to the program and not repeated. If you use a name that's already being used, like print, then you'll create a new definition that will overwrite the original one. This can cause some wild logic errors.

Section Eight — Subroutines

Defining Subroutines

Subroutines can contain nested statements

1) The quiz program will test the player on a particular times table by asking them to answer multiplications from '1 times' up to '12 times' a number — sounds like a for loop to me.
2) Handily, your subroutines can include all the good stuff like if statements, for loops, etc.

EXAMPLE Defining a subroutine to test a user's knowledge of the 7 times table.

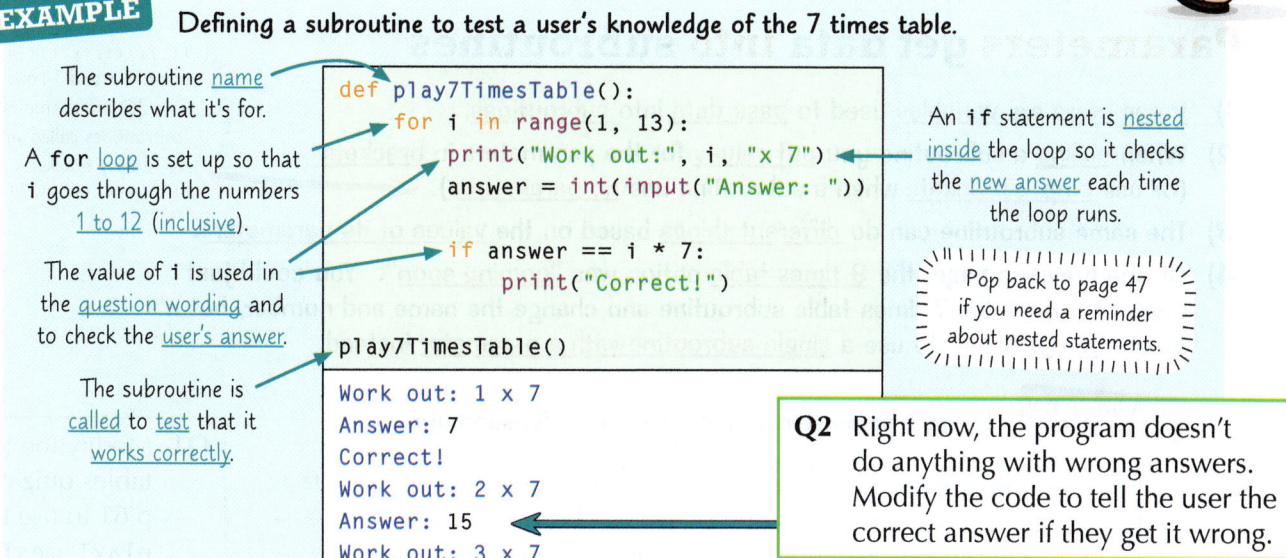

The subroutine name describes what it's for.

A for loop is set up so that i goes through the numbers 1 to 12 (inclusive).

The value of i is used in the question wording and to check the user's answer.

The subroutine is called to test that it works correctly.

An if statement is nested inside the loop so it checks the new answer each time the loop runs.

Pop back to page 47 if you need a reminder about nested statements.

Q2 Right now, the program doesn't do anything with wrong answers. Modify the code to tell the user the correct answer if they get it wrong.

Call subroutines in sequence to build a program

- All the subroutines needed for the times table quiz are defined — it's time to build the final program.
- For large programs like this, the subroutine definitions can go one after another at the start of the file.

EXAMPLE Combining user-defined subroutines to make the times tables quiz.

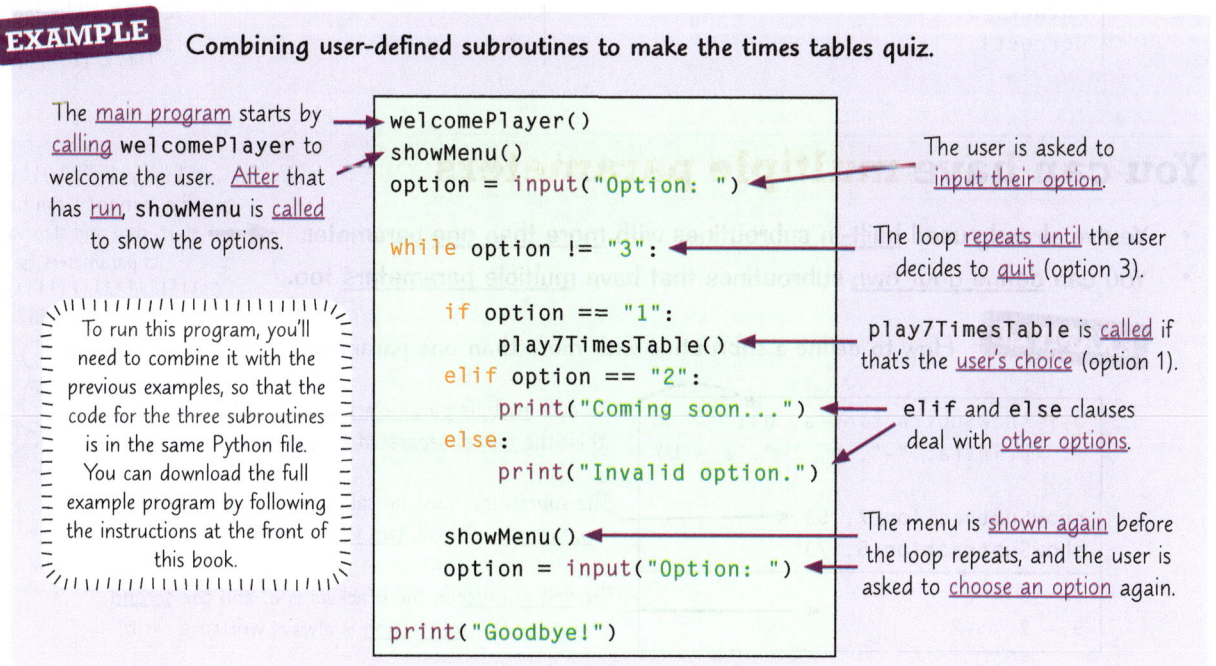

The main program starts by calling welcomePlayer to welcome the user. After that has run, showMenu is called to show the options.

To run this program, you'll need to combine it with the previous examples, so that the code for the three subroutines is in the same Python file. You can download the full example program by following the instructions at the front of this book.

The user is asked to input their option.

The loop repeats until the user decides to quit (option 3).

play7TimesTable is called if that's the user's choice (option 1).

elif and else clauses deal with other options.

The menu is shown again before the loop repeats, and the user is asked to choose an option again.

I've already defined what it means to be cool()...

Subroutines need to be defined before they are called. If you get an error saying a name is not defined, you may need to move the subroutine code above the line where it's being called.

Parameters

Learning Objectives

`print()` would be utterly useless if you couldn't give it the data you want to display. This is why parameters are needed — to supply subroutines with data to use.

- Understand the purpose of parameters.
- Be able to create a subroutine with one or more parameters.

Parameters get data into subroutines

1) Parameters are variables used to pass data into subroutines.
2) When calling a subroutine you put values for the parameters in brackets (or use empty brackets when a subroutine has no parameters).
3) The same subroutine can do different things based on the values of its parameters.
4) On the previous page, the 9 times table option was "coming soon". You could just copy and paste the 7 times table subroutine and change the name and number, but it's much more efficient to use a single subroutine with a parameter instead.

> .upper() and .lower() on p.20 are examples of subroutines called with empty brackets.

EXAMPLE Using a parameter to make a more useful subroutine.

```
def playTimesTable(n):
    for i in range(1, 13):
        print("Work out:", i, "x", n)
        answer = int(input("Answer: "))

        if answer == i * n:
            print("Correct!")

playTimesTable(9)
```
```
Work out: 1 x 9
Answer: 9
Correct!
```

To add a parameter, write a variable name in the brackets.

This is the same code as play7TimesTable() on the previous page, but with the parameter n replacing the 7s on these two lines.

The subroutine is called by giving a value for the parameter in the brackets.

Q1 Modify the times tables quiz on p.61 to use this `playTimesTable` subroutine to test both the 7 and 9 times table.

> This subroutine works not only for both the 7 and 9 times tables, but any other times table too.

You can have multiple parameters

- You've already used built-in subroutines with more than one parameter.
- You can define your own subroutines that have multiple parameters too.

> E.g. range() can have the start, stop and step values as its parameters (p.38)

EXAMPLE How to define a subroutine with more than one parameter.

```
def showSubtraction(a, b):
    print(a, "-", b, "=", a - b)

showSubtraction(7, 5)
showSubtraction(5, 7)
```
```
7 - 5 = 2
5 - 7 = -2
```

To add multiple parameters, simply add their the names separated by commas.

The subroutine must be called with a value for each parameter — here, two values need to be given.

The first number in the brackets is a, and the second one is b. The subtraction is always written a - b.

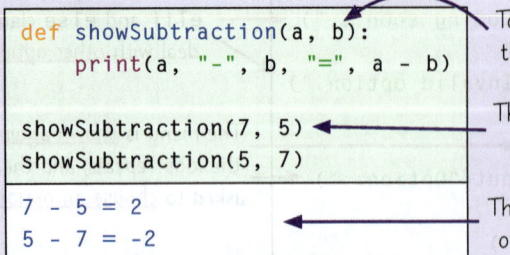

If Peter Python printed a pair of print parameters...

You may see Python error messages talking about 'arguments'. These are just the actual values that are passed into a subroutine when it's called — the values that the parameters take.

Section Eight — Subroutines

Return Values

Learning Objectives

`input()` would be utterly useless (this sounds familiar...) if it didn't give you the user's input. This is why return values are needed — so a subroutine can give you a result.

- Understand the purpose of return values.
- Be able to create a subroutine with a return value.

Return values get data out of subroutines

1) The quiz program on p.61 asked the user for input after every time it called `showMenu()`.
2) To avoid repeating code, you might be tempted to move the input line into the `showMenu` subroutine.
3) This is a reasonable idea, but it's not quite that simple...

```
showMenu()
option = input("Option: ")
```

COMMON PROBLEMS — Modifying `showMenu()` to get the user's input, then testing it works.

The variable `option` is now assigned inside the subroutine. But this means it can't be used outside the subroutine (even after the subroutine has run).

Variables that are defined inside the subroutine are not defined outside of it.

```
def getMenuChoice():
    print("Select an option (1-3).")
    print("1. Play 7 times table.")
    print("2. Play 9 times table.")
    print("3. Quit.")
    option = input("Option: ")

getMenuChoice()
print("Option", option, "selected.")
```

```
[after the menu is shown]
Option: 2
NameError: name 'option' is not defined
```

The subroutine name is changed to better match its new purpose.

This is an error, as the variable `option` doesn't exist in the main program.

Good return...

4) The solution to this problem is to use a return value — an output (or result) of a subroutine.
5) Like parameters are used to get data into a subroutine, a return value is used to get data out of a subroutine.

EXAMPLE — How to correctly return a value from a subroutine.

Write `return`, followed by the data you want to output — in this case, the value of `option`.

The returned value is assigned to a variable in the main program.

```
def getMenuChoice():
    print("Select an option (1-3).")
    print("1. Play 7 times table.")
    print("2. Play 9 times table.")
    print("3. Quit.")
    option = input("Option: ")
    return option

choice = getMenuChoice()
print("Option", choice, "selected.")
```

```
[after the menu is shown]
Option: 2
Option 2 selected.
```

GOING FURTHER — Subroutines can only have one return value, but you can use a data structure (p.50) to return more data if needed.

Q1 Modify the times tables quiz on p.61-62 to:
  a) Use `getMenuChoice()` instead of `showMenu()`.
  b) Have `welcomePlayer()` return the player's name and use it in the final "goodbye" message.

This may be crazy... but here's my function — call it, maybe?

Technically, a subroutine with a return value (such as `input`) is a "function", and a subroutine without a return value (such as `print`) is a "procedure", but Python doesn't make this distinction.

Practice Questions

Warm-Up
Q1 What feature of the code shows that a subroutine definition has ended?

Q2 True or false? Subroutine names can begin with a number, a letter or a symbol.

Q3 Which of the following list subroutines takes more than one parameter?

.append()   .insert()   .remove()

Q4 How many return values can a subroutine have?

Practice Questions

Q1 Describe how you can use 'decomposition' in programming.

....

....

Q2 Look at the program on the right below.

a) How many built-in subroutines are used?

....

```
def repeat(text, n):
    result = ""
    for i in range(n):
        result = result + text
    return result

word = input("Enter a word: ")
message = repeat(word, len(word))
print(message)
```

```
Enter a word: ha
```

```
Enter a word: haha
```

b) The program has a user-defined subroutine.

i) What is it called?

....

ii) What are the names of its parameters?

1. ....

2. ....

iii) What is the name of the return variable?

....

c) Complete the output for the two inputs shown above.

(ha ha ha ha
ha ha ha ha
ha ha ha ha)

Q3 Kira has modified the `playTimesTable` subroutine on page 62 so that it tracks how many answers the user gets correct and then returns that number.

```
def playTimesTable(n):
    score = ..........
    for i in range(1, 13):
        print("Work out:", i, "x", n)
        answer = int(input("Answer: "))
        if answer == i * n:
            print("Correct!")
            score = ..................... + 1
    .......................... score
```

a) Fill in the gaps to complete Kira's subroutine so that it behaves as described above.

b) Write two lines of code below to call the subroutine and then print the result.

Coding Challenges for Section Eight

Hold on, just gimme five and I'll return with a better joke... Eh never mind, I've got nothing. Try these challenges and don't forget to visit the link on the contents page to get example programs for each one.

Challenge 1 — Example

Write a subroutine that takes a list of numbers as input and then prints the smallest and the largest number in that list. Show your subroutine working on the following list: [5, 12, 6, -5, 10].

SOLUTION Plan: sort the list in ascending order, then the first and last items will be the smallest and the largest.

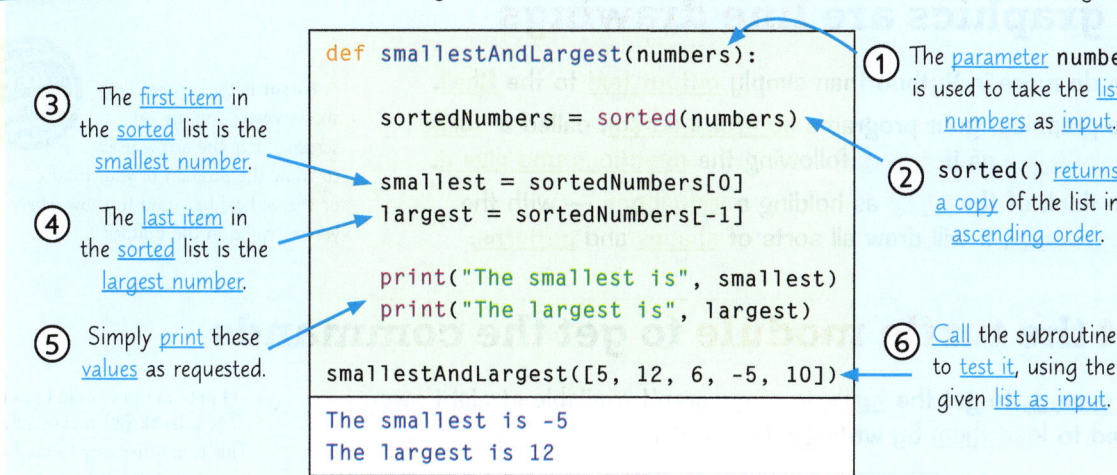

① The parameter numbers is used to take the list of numbers as input.
② sorted() returns a copy of the list in ascending order.
③ The first item in the sorted list is the smallest number.
④ The last item in the sorted list is the largest number.
⑤ Simply print these values as requested.
⑥ Call the subroutine to test it, using the given list as input.

```
def smallestAndLargest(numbers):

    sortedNumbers = sorted(numbers)

    smallest = sortedNumbers[0]
    largest = sortedNumbers[-1]

    print("The smallest is", smallest)
    print("The largest is", largest)

smallestAndLargest([5, 12, 6, -5, 10])
```

```
The smallest is -5
The largest is 12
```

Challenge 2

Write a subroutine that takes two numbers and returns the largest.

- Your subroutine should not use any built-in subroutines.
- Your subroutine should match the output shown on the right when called in the same way as shown in the code above.

```
print(largest(5, 8))
print(largest(0.7, 0.6))
print(largest(-4, -2))
print(largest(9, 9))
```
```
8
0.7
-2
9
```

Challenge 3

A dance club is doing a prize draw — one lucky member will win a new pair of tap shoes. You have been asked to write a program to help with the draw.

Your program should:

- Ask the user to enter names, one by one, adding each to a list of contenders.
- Stop taking names when the user enters "Draw!".
- Choose a random name from the list.
- Display a message revealing this name as the winner.

Video Solution

Challenge 4

Extend the program built on pages 60-63 to create Times Table Quiz: Deluxe Edition.
Your program should have three menu options:
1. Free choice — the user is asked to enter a number (1 to 12) to choose the times table they want to be tested on.
2. Random — the user is tested on a random times table (1 to 12).
3. Quit — ends the program.

Additionally, add some blank lines to the output to make it easier to read.

Section Eight — Subroutines

Section Nine — Turtle Graphics

Basic Commands

Learning Objectives

Imagine a turtle crawling along the page, holding a crayon. As it moves, its leaves its path traced onto the page — and for reasons known only to itself, it draws a perfect rectangle.

- Learn what turtle graphics are.
- Be able to import commands from the turtle module.
- Be able to use commands to move forwards and backwards.

Turtle graphics are line drawings

1) You can do more in Python than simply output text to the Shell.
2) In turtle graphics, your programs control a cursor, called a 'turtle', that draws a line as it moves following the directions you give it.
3) You can think of the turtle as holding a virtual pen — with the right commands, it will draw all sorts of shapes and patterns.

KEY TERMS
A **cursor** is the symbol that shows where you are on screen. E.g. the arrow used to show the position of your mouse, or the vertical bar used to show where you're typing in the Editor.

Import the turtle module to get the commands

- The commands to get the turtle to move aren't available straight away — you need to load them by writing this line at the start of your program:

  ```
  from turtle import *
  ```

- This loads all the subroutines from the turtle module.

The asterisk (*) means 'all'. This is another way to load a module (p.58). It lets you use all the turtle commands in your program without having to type out 'turtle.' before every one.

Draw lines by moving forwards and backwards

1) The `forward` command tells the turtle to move in a straight line in the direction it's currently facing.

   EXAMPLE How to move the turtle forwards.

   The number in the bracket tells it how many pixels to move.

   ```
   from turtle import *
   forward(100)
   ```

   When the program is run, a new window will pop up to show the drawing. The arrowhead shows the position of the turtle and the direction it's facing.

   KEY TERMS
   A **pixel** is the smallest square of colour in an image or on a screen.

   By default, the turtle starts off facing to the right, so it has moved 100 pixels right.

2) The `backward` command tells the turtle to move backwards in a straight line.

   EXAMPLE How to move the turtle backwards.

   The number in the bracket tells it how many pixels to move.

   ```
   from turtle import *
   backward(100)
   ```

   `backward()` moves the turtle in the opposite direction to where it's currently facing. So the turtle has moved 100 pixels left here, but stayed facing right.

   It's not as exciting as an actual turtle, but the arrow is useful for seeing which direction the turtle is facing.

Turtle graphics — ironically, bringing Python out of its Shell...

Having said that, typing commands directly into the Shell lets you see them play out one at a time, which is great for experimenting with this stuff. Just remember to write the `import` line first.

Simple Shapes

> **Learning Objectives**
> A drawing of a straight line isn't likely to be accepted into any art gallery — trust me, I've tried. To draw more interesting things, you'll need to learn how to turn the turtle.
> - Be able to use commands to turn left and turn right.
> - Be able to draw squares, triangles and other simple shapes.
> - Be able to hide, lift and lower the turtle.

Use angles to turn left or right

1) You can use commands to change the direction that the turtle is facing.
2) Use `left()` to turn left (anticlockwise) and `right()` to turn right (clockwise).
3) You put the angle to turn (in degrees) inside the brackets.

EXAMPLE Turn left and right to draw a simple path.

This turns the turtle right 60 degrees.

This turns the turtle left 40 degrees.

```
from turtle import *

forward(200)
right(60)
forward(120)
left(40)
forward(150)
```

The turtle follows the commands in order.

Put each command on a separate line or you'll get a syntax error.

Drawing a sketch can help you figure out whether a turn needs to go left or right.

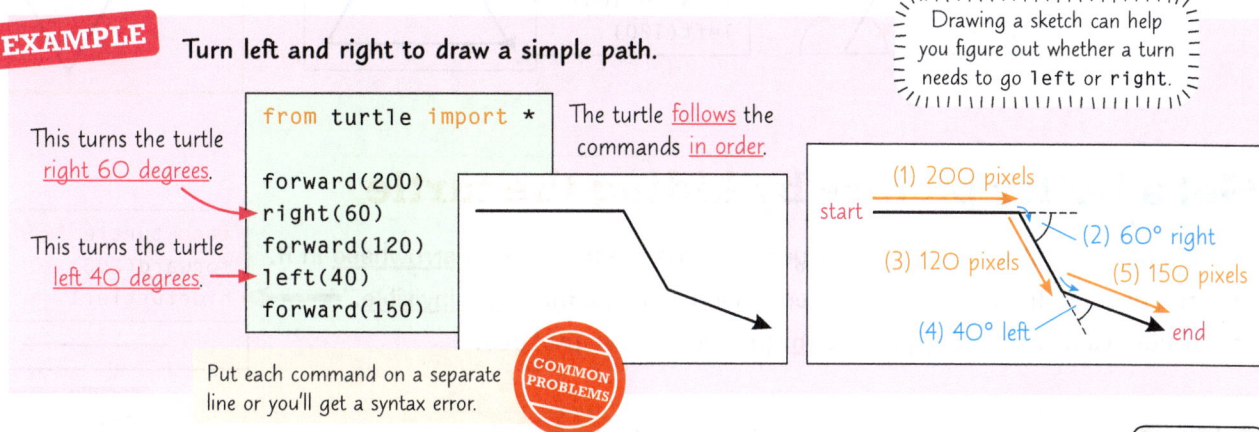

Turn 90 degrees to make square corners

You can create simple shapes, like squares and rectangles, by drawing a path that starts and ends at the same point.

EXAMPLE Drawing a square using `forward()` and `left()`.

```
from turtle import *

forward(200)
left(90)
forward(200)
```

This turtle turns left 90 degrees to make a square corner.

```
from turtle import *

forward(200)
left(90)
forward(200)
left(90)
forward(200)
left(90)
forward(200)
left(90)
```

This turtle makes four 90 degree turns to make a square. It ends up in the same place it began.

Q1 Write a turtle program to draw a rectangle with a width of 300 pixels and a height of 100 pixels.

Q2 Write a turtle program to draw the shape sketched below.

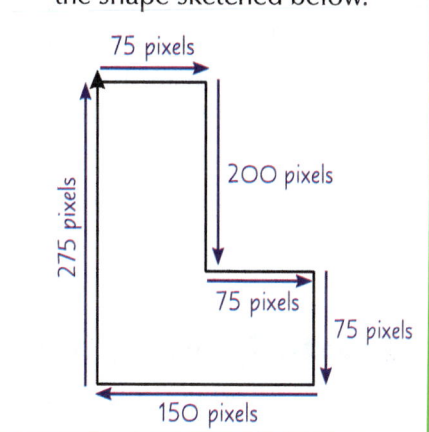

Simple Shapes

Turn 120 degrees to draw equilateral triangles

1) After squares and rectangles, naturally triangles are up next.
2) Equilateral triangles are the easiest to draw — they have three sides all the same length and three angles all the same size.

EXAMPLE Drawing an equilateral triangle.

The angles inside an equilateral triangle are 60 degrees, but it's the angles outside the triangle that you need to use.

See p.70 for more about drawing shapes like this.

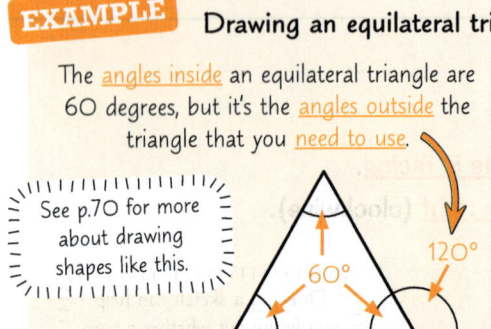
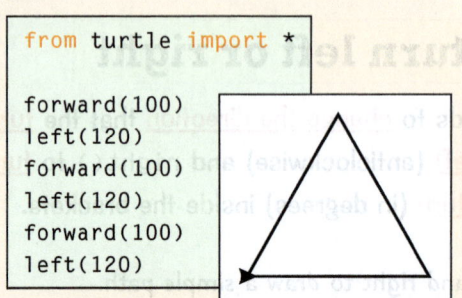

```
from turtle import *
forward(100)
left(120)
forward(100)
left(120)
forward(100)
left(120)
```

Q3 Write a program to draw an upside-down equilateral triangle like this:

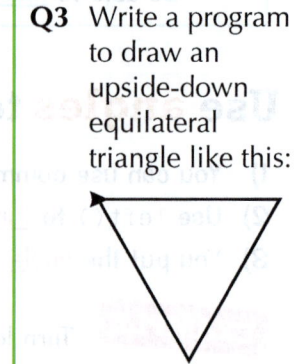

Get a better picture by hiding the turtle

- It's hard to get a nice picture of your art when you've got an arrowhead in it.
- You can use the hideturtle() command to make the turtle invisible.
- If you want to see the turtle again, just use showturtle().

```
from turtle import *
forward(200)
hideturtle()
_____
```

Lift the pen to move without drawing

1) At the moment, everywhere the turtle moves it draws a line.
2) You can stop the line being drawn by lifting the pen using penup().
3) You can start the line being drawn again by lowering the pen with pendown().

EXAMPLE Drawing horizontal parallel lines by lifting and lowering the pen.

Draw the first line. → `forward(300)`
Lift the pen up to stop drawing. → `penup()`
Get the turtle into position, ready to draw the second line. → `right(90)` `forward(100)` `right(90)`
Lower the pen down to start drawing again. → `pendown()`
Draw the second line, then hide the turtle. → `forward(300)` `hideturtle()`

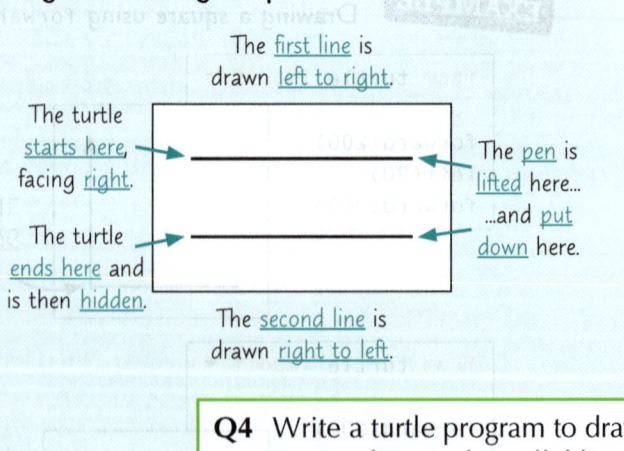

The first line is drawn left to right.
The turtle starts here, facing right.
The pen is lifted here… …and put down here.
The turtle ends here and is then hidden.
The second line is drawn right to left.

Q4 Write a turtle program to draw a pair of vertical parallel lines.

I turtally adore how you've captured the essence of that triangle…

There's a short version of each command — fd and bk for forward and backward, lt and rt for left and right, pu and pd for penup and pendown, and ht and st to hide and show the turtle.

Practice Questions

Warm-Up

Q1 At the start of a program:
   a) Which direction is the turtle facing?   b) Is the turtle shown or hidden?
   c) Is the pen up or down?

Q2 When moving the turtle forwards or backwards, what is the distance measured in?

Q3 True or false? When following a `backward` command, the turtle turns around before moving.

Q4 What command should be used to make the turtle turn a right-angle clockwise?

Practice Questions

Q1 Describe the purpose of the following lines of code.

Code	Description
`from turtle import *`	
`backward(150)`	
`left(20)`	

Q2 Write a program to draw the graphic shown below. Try to do it without lifting the pen or drawing over a line you've already drawn.

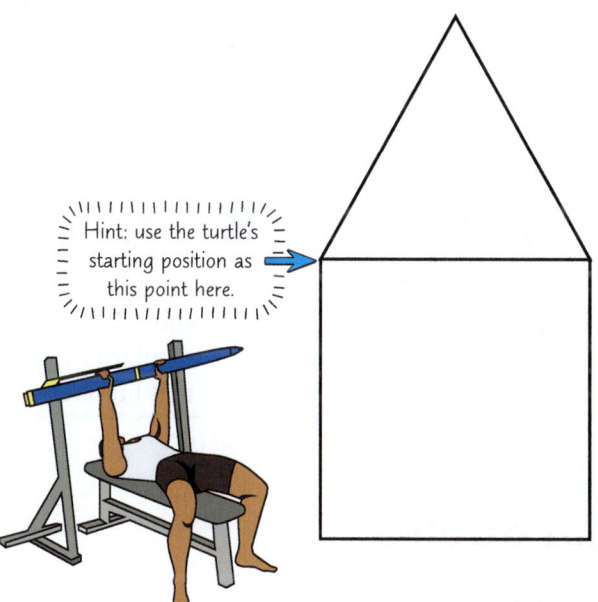

Hint: use the turtle's starting position as this point here.

```
from turtle import *
```

Q3 Without running the program below, draw what the output would look like.

```
from turtle import *

forward(100)
right(90)
penup()
forward(100)
left(90)
pendown()
forward(100)

hideturtle()
```

Section Nine — Turtle Graphics

Polygons and Circles

> **Learning Objectives**
>
> Pentagons, hexagons, icositetragons, etc., are the regular polygons. You know 'em, you love 'em and Python makes short work of 'em, provided you know a teensy bit of maths...
> - Be able to draw regular polygons with any number of sides.
> - Be able to draw circles.

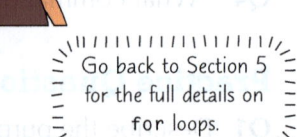

I–Icoth– Icothitethragon

Use for loops to draw regular polygons

1) The programs on p.67 and p.68 to draw squares and equilateral triangles weren't very efficient — they both repeated steps.
2) When you see code repeated like this, you should think about using a `for` loop.

Go back to Section 5 for the full details on `for` loops.

EXAMPLE Using a `for` loop to draw a square.

One side of the square is drawn each time the loop runs.

Turn the turtle so it's facing the right way to draw the next side.

```
from turtle import *
for i in range(4):
    forward(100)
    left(90)
hideturtle()
```

Q1 Write a program using a for loop to draw an equilateral triangle.

3) Squares and equilateral triangles are examples of regular polygons.
4) You can draw regular polygons with any number of sides.

KEY TERMS
A **polygon** is a shape with straight sides. A **regular** polygon is one where all the sides and angles are the same.

EXAMPLE A subroutine that draws regular polygons.

```
from turtle import *
def drawPolygon(n):
    for i in range(n):
        forward(100)
        left(360 / n)
drawPolygon(6)
hideturtle()
```

The parameter n is the number of sides.

This calculates the correct angle to turn. When n is 6, it's 360° ÷ 6 = 60°.

Q2 Write a program that asks the user for a number, then use this subroutine to draw a regular polygon with that number of sides.

There's a built-in command for circles

Because the turtle can only move forwards and backwards in straight lines, the only way to draw a circle is to draw a regular polygon with lots of really short sides. Conveniently, there's a built-in command just for this.

EXAMPLE Drawing a circle.

The number in brackets is the radius, in pixels.

```
from turtle import *
circle(100)
```

The circle command makes the turtle curve round to the left (anticlockwise).

Q3 Write a program to draw a snowman like the picture below.

Hint: draw the top circle first.

Polygons are prolly gonna be haunting my dreams tonight...

Programs that draw turtle graphics are still just regular Python code, so can include `if` statements, `for` loops, etc. There are some funky examples coming up that use the `random` module too.

Adding Colours

Learning Objectives

You can make a lot of moody art with just black and white, but sometimes a nice splash of colour is called for — here's how to add it.

- Be able to change the background colour of the turtle window.
- Be able to change the colour of a shape.
- Be able to change the colour and thickness of the pen.

You can add ~~colours~~ colors to turtle graphics

1) Turtle graphics don't need to be black and white — there are commands to add colour.
2) The `bgcolor` command sets the background window colour. The background is "White" by default.
3) There are a bunch of colour names you can use (too many to list here), including the main ones like "Red", "Green" and "Blue", and some odd ones like "MintCream" and "RosyBrown".

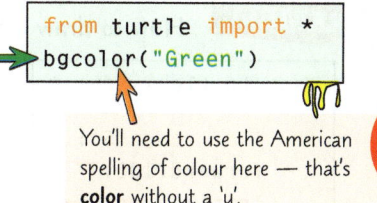

You'll need to use the American spelling of colour here — that's **color** without a 'u'.

There are four steps to colouring in shapes

Colouring shapes is a bit trickier but the steps are always the same.

EXAMPLE How to fill a shape with colour.

Step 1 — Set the fill colour by name. → `fillcolor("Yellow")`
Step 2 — Tell it to start filling before drawing the shape. → `begin_fill()`
Step 3 — Draw the shape. → `circle(100)`
Step 4 — Tell it to stop filling after the shape is drawn. → `end_fill()`
`hideturtle()`

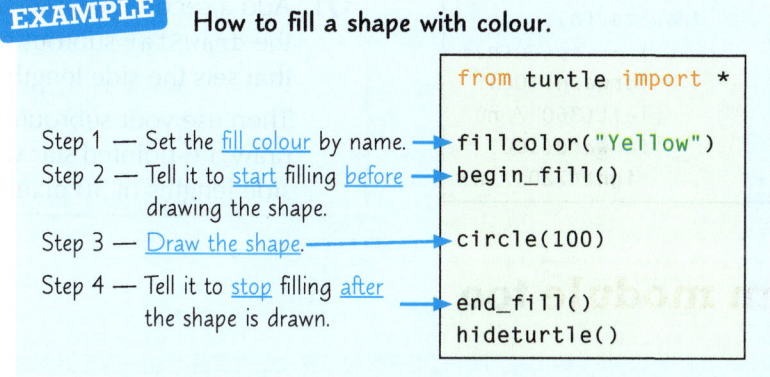

Q1 Write a program to draw this:

There are two ways to style the pen

You can use the `pensize` and `pencolor` commands to change how the line looks.

EXAMPLE Drawing a thick circle and colouring the line.

This sets the line thickness (in pixels). The higher the number, the thicker the line.

This sets the line colour. (pencolor is also spelt with no u).

```
from turtle import *
pensize(20)
pencolor("Magenta")
circle(100)
hideturtle()
```

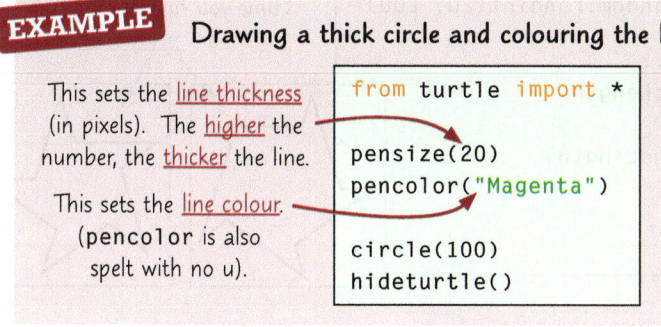

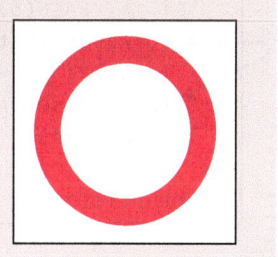

The pen starts with a size of 1 pixel and is coloured "black".

Q2 Write a program to draw this:

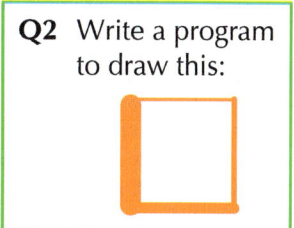

Startled-salmon pink isn't a usable colour? Who do I talk to...

Check out the downloadable files for this Section — colourNames.txt has a list of colour names that you can use in turtle graphics. My favourite is 'BlanchedAlmond' — that name is nuts.

Stars and Random Shapes

Learning Objectives

The best bit of turtle graphics is experimenting. The `random` module can really spice things up if you're feeling extra zany — you never know quite what you'll get.
- Be able to draw stars with any number of points.
- Learn how to use the `random` module with turtle graphics.

You need to turn both left and right to draw stars

1) There are many ways to draw a star shape, but one of the easiest is to use a similar method to the one for regular polygons (see p.70).

EXAMPLE How to draw a 5-pointed star.

```
from turtle import *

for i in range(5):
    forward(100)
    left(72)
    forward(100)
    right(144)

hideturtle()
```

The side lengths are all 100 pixels.

The turtle turns in different directions and by different amounts.

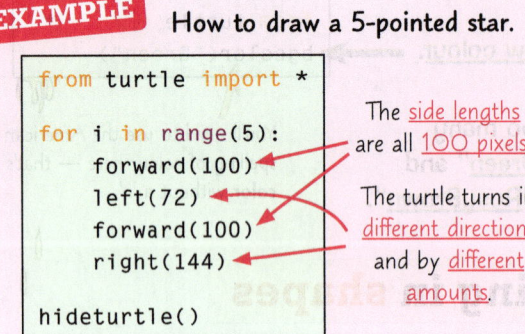

Throwin' random shapes

2) You can draw stars with any number of points using this subroutine — the parameter n is the number of points.

```
def drawStar(n):
    for i in range(n):
        forward(100)
        left(360 / n)
        forward(100)
        right(720 / n)
```

The value for n must be 5 or more.

Q1 Add a second parameter to the `drawStar` subroutine that sets the side length.

Then use your subroutine to draw a 6-pointed star with side lengths of 50 pixels.

You can use the random module too

EXAMPLE Using the `random` module to draw a random star.

You can use more than one module in the same program.

Use `.randint()` to get two random lengths.

This draws a 5-pointed star (like the example above) using the random lengths.

```
from turtle import *
import random

firstLength = random.randint(20, 200)
secondLength = random.randint(20, 200)

for i in range(5):
    forward(firstLength)
    left(72)
    forward(secondLength)
    right(144)

hideturtle()
```

As the `random` module has been imported like this, you need to write 'random.' before its subroutines.

You'll get a different star each time you run the program. Here are two possibilities.

You could change the two angles too, to get sharper or wider points, but you need to change both by the same amount, or the turtle won't start and end at the same point.

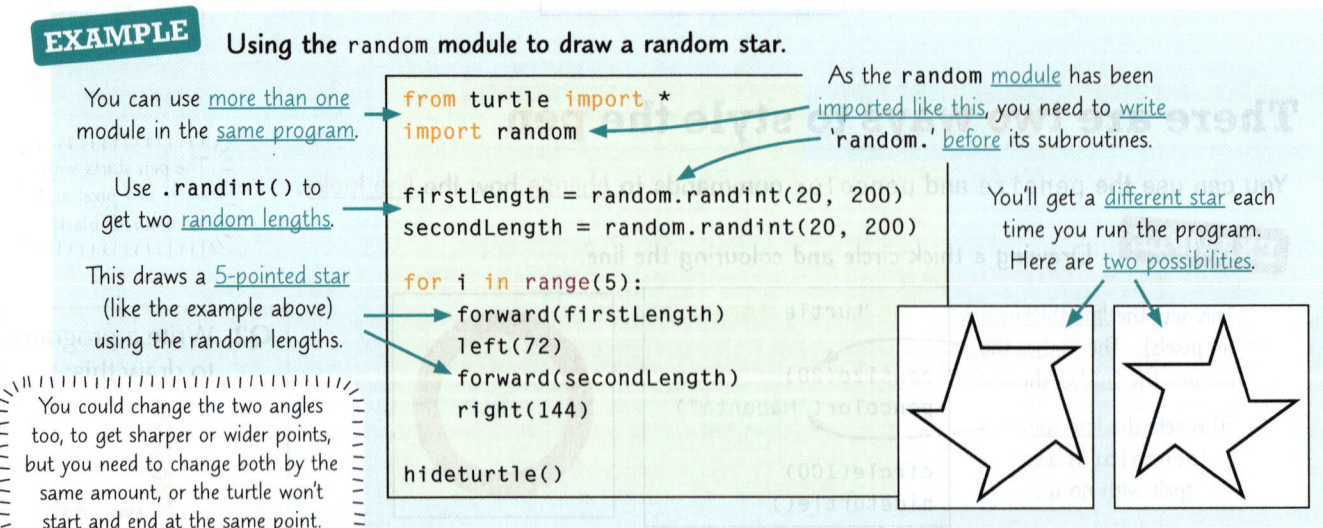

Leonardo, Michelangelo, Raphael, etc — the turtle all-stars...

These more complex shapes can be tricky to draw in turtle. If you can't figure out the angles, trial and error in the Shell may help — use the `undo()` command if you want to undo the last action.

Section Nine — Turtle Graphics

Practice Questions

Warm-Up

Q1 What does the number 100 represent in the command `circle(100)`?

Q2 What is wrong with the following line of code? ➡ `bgcolour("Red")`

Q3 Which command changes the thickness of the pen?

Q4 True or false? You can load more than one module at a time in the same program.

Practice Questions

Q1 Complete each program below so that they draw the graphics shown.

a)
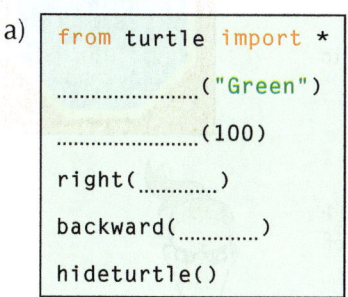

b)
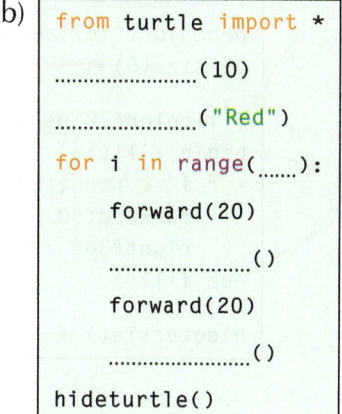
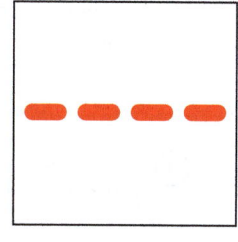

Q2 Martha would like a program that draws a regular polygon with a random number of sides (between 3 and 15, inclusive).

She wants the polygon to be on an "AliceBlue" coloured background and have a "PapayaWhip" fill.

Fill in the gaps on the right to complete this program.

```
from turtle import *
import ......................
......................("AliceBlue")
sides = random.......................(........, ........)
......................("........................")
begin_fill()
for i in range(......................):
    ......................(100)
    right(...................... / sides)
    ......................()
hideturtle()
```

Q3 Without running the program below, draw what the output would look like. The first line has been drawn for you.

```
from turtle import *

angle = int(input("Enter angle: "))

for i in range(3):
    forward(100)
    left(angle)
    backward(100)
    right(angle)

hideturtle()

Enter angle: 50
```

Section Nine — Turtle Graphics

Coding Challenges for Section Nine

Time for another set of challenges — these are all about how well you can control that metaphorical turtle. Paint your best pictures, then visit the link on the contents page for example programs for each one.

Challenge 1 — Example

Write a program to draw an octagon with a thick yellow outline and a blue fill, on a crimson background.

SOLUTION Plan: set the colours and then use a for loop to draw one side at a time.

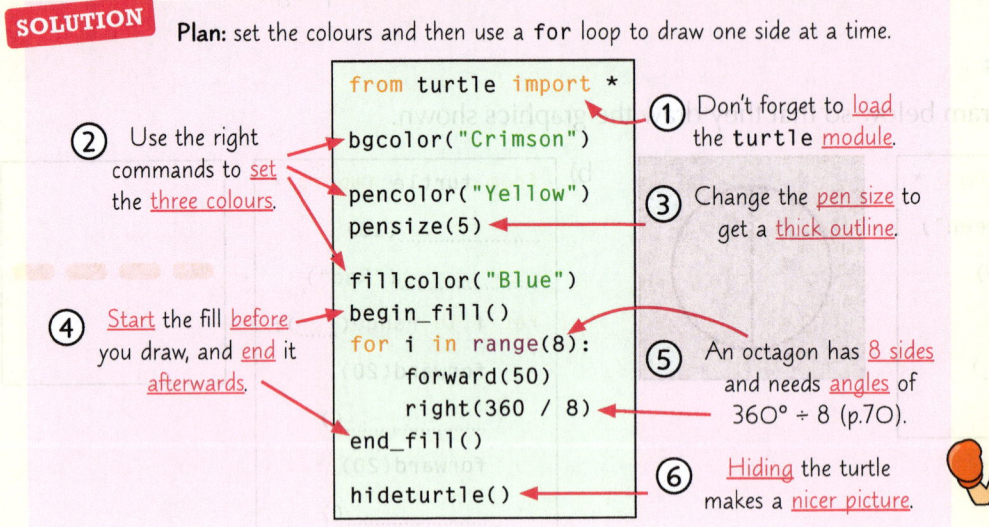

② Use the right commands to set the three colours.

① Don't forget to load the turtle module.

③ Change the pen size to get a thick outline.

④ Start the fill before you draw, and end it afterwards.

⑤ An octagon has 8 sides and needs angles of 360° ÷ 8 (p.70).

⑥ Hiding the turtle makes a nicer picture.

```
from turtle import *
bgcolor("Crimson")
pencolor("Yellow")
pensize(5)
fillcolor("Blue")
begin_fill()
for i in range(8):
    forward(50)
    right(360 / 8)
end_fill()
hideturtle()
```

Hint: turtle can take foreeeever with big drawings. To speed things up, you can add the command speed(0) to your program (at the top, after all modules are imported).

Challenge 2

Chandra, Charlie and Chang have made the logo on the right for their letter C appreciation club.

Write a program to draw this logo.
The C's have a 'Red' outline and a 'LightPink' fill.

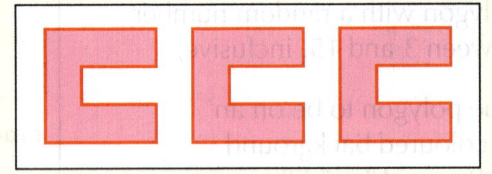

Challenge 3

Write a program to draw a stick person like the one shown on the right. Give the body a random height.

Hint: if you backtrack over a line you've already drawn, you can avoid lifting and lowering the pen.

Challenge 4

A maths teacher wants a program they can use to show their pupils different shapes. An example of the program's menu is shown on the right.

Your program should:
- Ask the pupil which shape they would like to see: polygon, star or circle.
- For the first two options, ask them how many sides or points they want.
- Draw that shape with a side length, or radius, of 50 pixels.

```
Choose a shape to see.
1. Polygon
2. Star
3. Circle
Enter option: 2
```

Challenge 5

Rosie has sketched a design on the right, and made a list of her favourite colours.

Write a program to draw Rosie's design.
Fill each triangle with a random colour from the list.

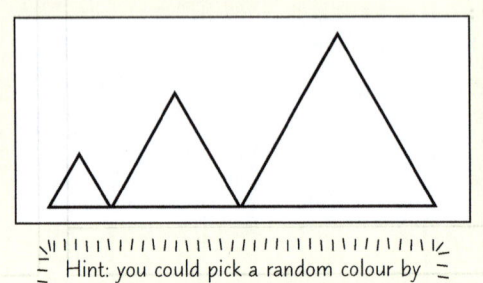

Hint: you could pick a random colour by generating a random index for the list.

My Favourite Colours
- Aqua
- Bisque
- Coral
- DarkOrchid
- Fuchsia
- GhostWhite
- HoneyDew

Video Solution

Section Nine — Turtle Graphics

Section Ten — Longer Challenges

Worked Challenges

It's time to bring together everything you've learned so far. These coding challenges will test your knowledge across multiple topics. They may take longer than the earlier challenges, but if you've covered everything in the book so far, then you'll be perfectly primed to take them on — good luck and godspeed, programmer.

Some last-minute advice

When the program works. When the program doesn't work.

Oh wait, before you start, here are a few pointers:
1) Read the challenges carefully before jumping into IDLE.
2) A bit of planning up front can prevent headaches later on.
   - Break down the problem into the smaller tasks that need doing (p.60).
   - Code one part at a time — there's usually an easier task you can start with to get going.
   - For the trickier tasks, consider drawing a flowchart or writing some pseudocode (p.8).
3) Save copies of your work regularly and use a new file name for bigger changes.
   That way you can go back to an older version if you need to.
4) Run your code frequently to test it, so you can fix any errors as soon as they creep in.
   Don't get put off by errors — they're always going to happen. Keep calm and fix them.
5) If you've forgotten how to do something, look back in the book and have a recap.

Here are some example challenges to get you going. Have a go yourself, then see the next page for how you could do them. Don't forget to visit the link on the contents page to download code files for all the challenges.

Worked Challenge 1 — Takeaway Kiosk

Tyrone is installing a self-service kiosk at his takeaway restaurant. It needs to be programmed to process orders. They sell chicken nuggets at 50p per piece and dipping sauces at 20p per pot.

Write a program to:
- Ask the user how many nuggets and how many dips they want.
- Display the total cost (in £) of the order to the user.
- Ask the user to enter an amount of money.
- Display how much change the user will get, or how much extra they need to pay.

GOING FURTHER: Use the built-in subroutine format() to display amounts of money in the correct format, e.g. format(1.5, ".2f") returns the string "1.50".

Worked Challenge 2 — Generating Usernames

An online game has become very popular and new players are having trouble signing up because the most common usernames have already been taken.

To help with this problem, you've been asked to write a program to generate usernames that can be suggested to new players. Using a list of animal names and random 4-digit numbers, your program should generate usernames in the form 'animal####' (e.g. iguana4031).

Show that your program works by printing 5 username suggestions.

Worked Challenge 3 — Drawing a Seashell

Sian's seaside shack sells 3-scoop ice creams using seashells as containers. She has designed the image on the right to advertise her 'Dessert of the Day'.

Write a program to draw the seashell in Sian's design. It consists of nine circles alternating in two colours.

Hint: think about the order you need to draw the shapes.

GOING FURTHER: Extend your program to draw the three scoops of ice cream too. Allow Sian to choose the three colours used.

Worked Challenges

Worked Challenge 1 — Takeaway Kiosk

SOLUTION Plan: use casting to process to user input and an `if` statement to give the appropriate response.

① The numbers of nuggets and dips are whole numbers, so the user's inputs are converted to integers.

② The total cost is calculated in pounds, so the numbers are multiplied by floats, e.g. 0.5 represents 50p = £0.50.

③ The amount of money is cast to a float as the user may enter a decimal number.

④ The `if` condition is used to decide which response to give.

```
nuggets = int(input("How many nuggets? "))
dips = int(input("How many dips? "))

cost = nuggets * 0.5 + dips * 0.2

print("That'll be £" + str(cost))
amount = float(input("Enter money: £"))

if amount >= cost:
    print("Here's £" + str(amount - cost) + " in change.")
else:
    print("You're £" + str(cost - amount) + " short.")
```

Worked Challenge 2 — Generating Usernames

SOLUTION Plan: use the `randint()` function from the `random` module to get the random behaviour.

① Don't forget to load the `random` module.

② Set the list of animals — you could add more.

③ You've been asked to print 5 usernames, so set up a loop to repeat 5 times.

④ Choose a random index and use it to pick an animal from the list.

⑤ A four-digit number is an integer from 1000 to 9999 (inclusive).

⑥ Convert the number to a string and concatenate it to the animal name.

⑦ Finally, output the name to the Shell.

```
import random

animals = ["axolotl", "badger", "echidna", "ferret",
           "iguana", "python", "rabbit", "tortoise"]

for i in range(5):
    randomIndex = random.randint(0, len(animals) - 1)
    randomAnimal = animals[randomIndex]
    randomNumber = random.randint(1000, 9999)
    username = randomAnimal + str(randomNumber)
    print(username)
```

Worked Challenge 3 — Drawing a Seashell

SOLUTION Plan: draw the circles inside a `for` loop, using the loop variable as the radius of the circles.

① Import the turtle module this way to make all the commands easier to use.

② The `for` loop is set up so the loop variable can be used as the radius of the circles.

③ Count down so that the largest circle is drawn first, so it's at the back, and each smaller circle is drawn on top.

④ Use the 'four steps' (p.71) to draw a coloured circle.

⑤ An `if` statement is used to alternate the colour at the end of each loop.

⑥ The turtle is hidden so the arrow doesn't show.

Remember, you could add the command `speed(0)` if you want the turtle to draw quicker.

```
from turtle import *

colour = "Bisque"
for radius in range(100, 10, -10):
    fillcolor(colour)
    begin_fill()
    circle(radius)
    end_fill()
    if colour == "Bisque":
        colour = "Coral"
    else:
        colour = "Bisque"
hideturtle()
```

Independent Challenges

Time for the proper bit. These challenges are designed to make you think, but each have easier bits so have a go at all of them. These first four challenges mostly focus on content from Sections 1 to 4.

Challenge 1 — Merits and Demerits

A school uses a points system to reward pupils for good behaviour.
- A merit (+1 point) is given for good behaviour, like working hard in a lesson.
- A demerit (−1 point) is given for bad behaviour, like missing the colon off an `if` statement.

A program is needed to work out the overall points at the end of a year, and determine the award each pupil has earned. Example output is shown in the code box below.

The awards are decided using this table.

Overall Points	Award
100 or more	An LED gamer keyboard.
45 to 99	An afternoon of board games.
20 to 44	A free lunch token.
19 or fewer	A talking-to.

```
Enter name: Dennis
How many merits did they get? 103
How many demerits did they get? 68
Dennis has 35 points.
They've earned a free lunch token.
```

Not acceptable

Challenge 2 — Meme Generator

Write a program that can generate ASCII memes. Two example meme formats are shown on the right.

Your program should:
- Ask the user to choose a format from a menu of options.
- Ask the user to enter the text that they want to be displayed.
- Print the chosen meme with the user's text inserted.

```
Top text: for loops
Bottom text: while loops

    %%%%       |
   ( - - )     | for loops
    )^ ( |    |
   <    \/    |
---------------------------
    %%%%       |
   ( ^_^)     | while loops
    )  ( b    |
   \_b /      |
```

```
First text: if statements
Second text: elif clauses
Third text: else clauses

   / _ _\     |
  (> o o )    | if statements
   ) v (      |
---------------------------
   / - -\     |
  (> @ @ )    | elif clauses
   ) V (      |
---------------------------
   / ` `\     |
  (> ^ ^ )    | else clauses
   ) 0 (      |
```

Templates for these two formats can be found in the memes.txt file in the downloadable files for this section.

Challenge 3 — Data Units Converter

Computers store data using 0s and 1s, where each 0 or 1 is called a bit. 8 bits in a row is called a byte. When you have 1000 bytes you have a kilobyte, and then 1000 kilobytes is a megabyte.

Write a program that can convert between bits and megabytes.
Your program should display a menu giving the user two options:
1) Convert bits.
2) Convert megabytes.

Extend your program to allow the user to convert from bytes and kilobytes too.

It should then ask for the number of bits/megabytes to convert, then show it in terms of the other units (making sure to always give bits as an integer). Here are example conversions that you can use to test.

```
Enter a whole number of bits: 8000
8000 bits is the same as:
- 1000.0 bytes
- 1.0 kilobytes
- 0.001 megabytes
```

```
Enter a number of megabytes: 16.2
16.2 megabytes is the same as:
- 129600000 bits
- 16200000.0 bytes
- 16200.0 kilobytes
```

Section Ten — Longer Challenges

Independent Challenges

Challenge 4 — Letter Frequencies

The tables below show how often letters occur in English. For example, the letter 'a' has a frequency of 8.31% — this means an average of about 8 in every 100 letters is an 'a'.

Letter	Frequency (%)
a	8.31
b	1.46
c	3.02
d	4.15
e	12.93
f	2.03
g	2.21
h	5.94
i	7.12
j	0.22
k	0.68
l	4.07
m	2.32

Letter	Frequency (%)
n	6.89
o	7.54
p	1.77
q	0.11
r	6.09
s	6.92
t	7.15
u	2.74
v	0.80
w	2.49
x	0.92
y	1.56
z	0.56

Write a program that:
- Lets you to enter: a sentence, a letter and the expected frequency of that letter from the table.
- Calculates the actual frequency of the letter in the sentence by dividing how many times the letter appears by the total number of letters, then multiplying by 100.

  Assume the sentence only contains letters and spaces, and don't count the spaces.

- Then tells you whether the actual frequency of the letter is about as expected (i.e. within 1% of the expected frequency), or higher or lower than expected.

GOING FURTHER — Store the data in the tables as a 2D list in your program. Then instead of asking the user to enter the letter, loop through all 26 letters in the list and display a message for each one.

These next four challenges mostly practice content from Sections 5 and 6.

Challenge 5 — I Have A Secret

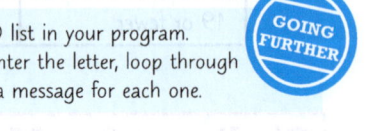

Write a program for a two-player game based on the following rules.

- Player 1 is asked to enter a secret word.
  To make this fair, Player 2 should be asked to look away. After Player 1 has entered their word, the command `print("\n")` should be repeated 50 times so the word is hidden from the screen.
- Player 2 is asked to look back and starts guessing:
  - First they enter a letter and are told how many times it appears in the secret word. Your program should not allow them to enter more than a single letter.
  - They then guess the secret word. If they get it wrong, they're allowed to ask about another letter and take another guess. This should repeat until they guess correctly.
- Once they guess the correct word, tell them how many guesses it took.

Challenge 6 — Team Selection

In an online multiplayer game, at the start of a match, a team must pick four characters to play as.

The characters are grouped into four classes, and only one choice can be made from each class. The characters are shown in the table on the right.

Due to balance concerns, players cannot pick both Elizmendi and Marpessa on the same team.

Fighter	Ranger	Magician	Rogue
Godusa	Huguet	Elizmendi	Juhota
Woco	Chryseida	Amadeus	Marpessa
Rikmai		Sibbe	Alan
		Cometus	

Write a program to:
- Ask the user to pick one character from each class in turn.
- If they enter an invalid option or break a selection rule, then ask them to pick again.
- Once all characters are chosen, output the final choices.

GOING FURTHER — Write a team selection program that allows the classes to be picked in any order, and displays a list of available characters for each pick. You can use 'in' to test if a character is in a list, e.g. `if "Marpessa" in characters:`

Section Ten — Longer Challenges

Independent Challenges

Challenge 7 — Rate My Password

Saige's computer has been hacked one too many times. She wants a program to rate the strength of her passwords based on the following point system.

- **+1 point** for each character **more than 5** it has, up to a **maximum of +7**.
  E.g. an 8-character password would get +3 points.
- **−1 point** for each character **fewer than 5** it has.
  E.g. a 3-character password would get −2 points.
- **+2 points** for every **symbol** ("@", "!" or "#") it has, up to a **maximum of +6**.
  Each symbol can score **more than once**, e.g. "@@" would get +4 points.
- **−5 points** if it's **entirely lowercase** or **entirely uppercase**.

Video Solution

Write a program to rate passwords based on Saige's system.
It should output the points total, and one of these messages:

- **10 or more points**: Strong password — accepted.
- **5-9 points**: Medium strength — accepted, but try better next time.
- **Less than 5 points**: Weak password — rejected.

GOING FURTHER: Turn your program into a password rating subroutine, then repeatedly ask the user to enter a password until one is accepted by the subroutine.

These final four challenges mostly practice content from Sections 7 to 9.

Challenge 8 — FizzBuzz

FizzBuzz is a maths activity that involves counting up, but saying "**Fizz**" instead of any **multiple of 3**, "**Buzz**" instead of any **multiple of 5**, and "**FizzBuzz**" instead of any **multiple of both 3 and 5** (i.e. any multiple of 15).

Write a program that shows the **FizzBuzz sequence** up to 100.

- Use this line of code to create a **list** of the numbers **1 to 100** (inclusive).
- Replace the appropriate numbers in the list with "**Fizz**", "**Buzz**" or "**FizzBuzz**" according to the **rules above**.
- **Display the sequence** like the example output on the right.

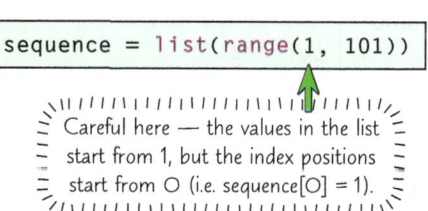

```
sequence = list(range(1, 101))
```

Careful here — the values in the list start from 1, but the index positions start from 0 (i.e. sequence[0] = 1).

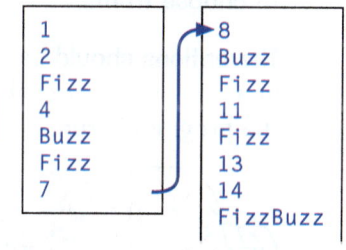

```
1         8
2         Buzz
Fizz      Fizz
4         11
Buzz      Fizz
Fizz      13
7         14
          FizzBuzz
```

GOING FURTHER: Allow the user to set which two words (e.g. "Fizz" and "Buzz") and which two prime numbers (e.g. 3 and 5) are used to generate the sequence.

Challenge 9 — Snake Latin

You may have heard of 'Pig Latin' — this is similar, but with a Python twist.

Snake Latin is a **fake language** in which **English words** are **changed** by the following rules:
- If a word **begins with a vowel**, then "**sssay**" is added to the end.
- Otherwise, the **first letter** is moved to the end and followed by "**ay**".

For example, "integer" would become "integersssay" and "float" would become "loatfay".

Create a **subroutine** that **translates** any given English word into a **Snake Latin word**.

Show your subroutine works by **testing** it on the words: "wake", "up", "it's", "coding", "time".

GOING FURTHER: The .split() method can break up a string into a list of words, e.g. "snake latin".split(" ") gives the list ["snake", "latin"]. Use this to translate any sentence entered by the user into Snake Latin.

Section Ten — Longer Challenges

Independent Challenges

Challenge 10 — Hot or Cold

Create a game of 'Hot or Cold' using turtle graphics. The aim of the game is for the player to find hidden treasure by moving the turtle to the correct position on the screen.

- Your program should store a pair of coordinates representing where some treasure is hidden in the turtle window — the centre is (0, 0).

```
treasure = (150, -250)
```
Set the coordinates of the treasure like this.

Distance (pixels)	Message
> 300	Ice cold
> 200 but ≤ 300	Cold
> 100 but ≤ 200	Warm
> 50 but ≤ 100	Very warm!
> 20 but ≤ 50	HOT!!
≤ 20	You found it!

Suggested hints that check() could give.

- The game is played by the user entering commands into the Shell.
- The usual commands (forward(), left(), etc) from the turtle module should be used to move the turtle around.
- A user-defined subroutine, check(), should say if the treasure has been found or else give a hint about how close the turtle is to it.

```
dist = distance(treasure)
```
Find how close the turtle is to the treasure like this.

GOING FURTHER — Extend the check() subroutine to draw a circle at the turtle's position, with a colour depending on how close the turtle is to the treasure, e.g. DeepSkyBlue for 'Ice cold'.

Challenge 11 — Python Quiz

Ms. Hissington is fed-up with pupils copying each other's answers. She has decided for her next multiple-choice quiz, pupils will be given answer options in different orders. From a web search, she has found that the random module has a .shuffle() function that mixes up the items in a given list.

Create a program that asks the user a multiple-choice question.

The user should be given four answer options to choose from.

The options should be shown in a random order each time the program is run.

```
A 'for' loop is an example of a ...?
1) condition-controlled loop
2) counter-culture loop
3) count-controlled loop
4) remote-controlled loop
Answer (1-4): 3
Correct!
```

```
import random
things = ["A", "B", "C"]
print("Before:", things)
random.shuffle(things)
print("After:", things)

Before: ['A', 'B', 'C']
After: ['B', 'C', 'A']
```

GOING FURTHER — Turn your program into a full quiz that asks multiple questions — one for each section of this book, perhaps. Make sure you have a way of remembering which option is correct before you shuffle them up.

Challenge 12 — Shortest and Longest

Python has two built-in functions, min() and max(), that can be used to find the shortest or longest items from a list of strings, like this.

```
words = ["his", "cat", "wears", "pyjamas", "to", "bed"]
print(min(words, key=len))
print(max(words, key=len))

to
pyjamas
```
Don't worry about understanding this code — it's advanced stuff.

You're challenged to define two subroutines yourself, shortest() and longest(), that each take a list of strings and return the shortest or longest string in the list (picking the one that appears first in the list if there's a tie).

```
print(shortest(words))
print(longest(words))

to
pyjamas
```

The catch is, you're not allowed to use any built-in subroutines except for len().

Test your program on the example code above.

GOING FURTHER — Define smallest() and biggest() that find the smallest and biggest integers in a list. Then define newMin() and newMax() that take either a list of strings or a list of integers and calls the appropriate subroutines. To check the data type of a variable, you can use e.g. type(x) == str.

Section Ten — Longer Challenges

Quick Reference Guide

Built-in Subroutines

Python has lots of handy subroutines you can use — here are the main ones used throughout this book.

Name	Description	Example
`print()`	Outputs a message to the Shell.	`print("Hello, world!")`
`input()`	Gets user input from the Shell.	`reply = input("What's up?")`
`str()`	Converts a value to a string.	`str(123)` is `"123"`
`int()`	Converts a value to an integer (whole number).	`int(3.4)` is `3`
`float()`	Converts a value to a float (decimal).	`float("4")` is `4.0`
`len()`	Returns the length of a string (number of characters) or list (number of items).	`len("banana bread")` is `12` `len(["a", "b", "c"])` is `3`
`range()`	Generates a sequence of numbers that can be used in e.g. a for loop. Can take a start, stop and step value.	`range(6)` is `0, 1, 2, 3, 4, 5` `range(0, 10, 3)` is `0, 3, 6, 9`
`.lower()`	When used on a string, returns the string in all lowercase.	`"AbCd".lower()` is `"abcd"`
`.upper()`	When used on a string, returns the string in all uppercase.	`"aBcD".upper()` is `"ABCD"`
`.count()`	When used on a string, tells you how many times a character (or another string) appears in it.	`"banana bread".count("a")` is `4` `"banana bread".count("an")` is `2`
`.append()`	When used on a list, adds an item to the end of the list.	`letters = ["a", "b"]` `letters.append("c")`
`.insert()`	When used on a list, puts an item at a particular index (position) in the list.	`letters = ["a", "c"]` `letters.insert(1, "b")`
`.remove()`	When used on a list, deletes an item from the list.	`letters = ["a", "b", "c"]` `letters.remove("c")`

Common Errors

Python has special names for some errors — the ones you're likely to bump into are listed below.

Name	When it occurs	Example
`NameError`	When you've used a variable or function name that doesn't exist (e.g. before it's defined), or when you've simply misspelled it.	`print(number)` `number = 5`
`TypeError`	When a value has the wrong data type for what you're trying to do with it.	`age = "nine"` `older = age + 5`
`IndentationError`	When indentation in your code isn't correct. (IDLE will usually spot this as a syntax error.)	`for i in range(5):` `print(i)`
`ZeroDivisionError`	When you've tried to divide a number by 0.	`result = 5 / 0`
`IndexError`	When you've tried to access a list item, or string character, using an index that doesn't exist.	`letters = ["a", "b"]` `print(letters[2])`
`SyntaxError`	When you try to run your code but you've written something that Python can't interpret.	`print("oops)`

Glossary

Glossary of Useful Words

There are loads of words used in Python that you may not be familiar with — here are some of them.

Algorithm		A set of step-by-step instructions to solve a problem.
Arithmetic operator		Used for basic maths — adding (+), subtracting (-), multiplying (*), dividing (/).
Block		A section of related code. The main types are: sequence, selection and iteration.
Boolean		The data type with two values: True or False.
Boolean operator		The operators used on Boolean values to give Boolean results — and, or, not.
Casting		The process of converting from one data type to another.
Character		A single letter, digit, space or symbol.
Clause		Can refer to else clauses or elif clauses — the optional parts of if statements.
Concatenation		Joining together pieces of text, one after the other.
Condition		An expression controlling an if statement, an elif clause or a while loop.
Data structure		An organised collection of items stored under one name — e.g. a list.
Data type		A kind of data — the four main ones in Python are: string, integer, float and Boolean.
Decomposition		Breaking a bigger problem down into smaller problems.
Editor window		The IDLE window where you write, edit and save programs.
Escape character		A special character that changes how text is displayed (e.g. \n gives a new line).
Float		The data type for any number written with a decimal point.
IDLE		An integrated development environment (IDE) that comes free with Python.
Indent		A gap at the beginning of a line of code.
Index		A number that specifies the position of a character in a string, or an item in a list.
Integer		The data type for whole numbers.
Iteration		Used to repeat a block of code a number of times.
List		A data structure that's simply an ordered sequence of values.
Logic error		An error that causes a program to do something that wasn't intended.
Nesting		When one statement is put inside another — e.g. an if statement in a while loop.
Parameter		A variable used to pass data into a subroutine.
Pseudocode		Fake code written in the style of a programming language, often to draft a program.
Relational operator		Used to compare values — always returns a Boolean value (True or False).
Selection		Used to write code that has multiple paths and react to user input and variables.
Sequence		Used for logical step-by-step code that runs line by line from top to bottom.
Shell Window		The IDLE window where you see the input and output of programs.
String		The data type for a collection of characters.
Subroutine		A named block of code that performs a particular task — is only run when called.
Syntax error		An error in a program caused by breaking the rules of the programming language.
Variable		A name used in a program that holds a value.

Answers

Section One — Introducing Python

Page 2 — What is Python?
Q1 E.g. Amazon, Disney®, Mozilla, Pixar, Uber, YouTube™

Page 4 — The Shell Window
Q1 a) 35
b) 68461

Page 7 — Your First Program
Q1 #learningtocode
Let's go!!
Each print command puts the text on a new line.

Q2 `PRINT("Bounjour le monde")`
print should be lowercase.

`print("Hola Mundo"])`
A round bracket should be used, not a square bracket.

`prinnt("Konnichiwa sekai")`
print is misspelled.

Page 8 — Algorithms
Q1
1) Mix the dough
2) Shape the dough
3) Put in fryer
4) Take out of fryer
5) Glaze with icing
6) Take a bite

Page 9 — Warm-Up
Q1 True
Q2 .py
Q3 A syntax error.
Q4 Input and output

Page 9 — Practice Questions
Q1 E.g. any 3 of:
- Desktop computer
- Laptop computer
- Mini-computer
- Tablet
- Smartphone
- Graphing calculator

Q2 Programs written in the Editor can be saved so you can come back to them later. The Shell is only really appropriate for simple programs that don't need to be saved.

Q3 E.g. any 3 of:
- Auto-indentation
- Code completion tips
- Visual customisation
- Syntax highlighting
- Error checking

Q4

Python Code	Syntax Error?
`print("Paris is the UK capital.")`	No
`print(^Hello, world^)`	Yes
`PRINT("What is your age?")`	Yes
`print("I am -13 years old.")`	No

Q5 a) An algorithm is a set of instructions for how to do something. A program is the computer code used to carry out those instructions.
b) Pseudocode is used to a draft a program without worrying about the syntax of a real programming language.

Section Two — Outputs, Inputs and Variables

Page 10 — Printing on Screen
Q1 `print("One function in the bag!")`
Q2 Line 3 is correct.
Line 1 is incorrect: 'Print' should not have a capital P.
Line 2 is incorrect: a quotation mark is missing before the last bracket.
Line 4 is incorrect: the quotation marks should be inside the brackets.

Page 11 — Collecting User Input
Q1 E.g.
```
print("Hello there.")
input("What is your name?")
input("And how are you feeling?")
print("Super. Chat again soon.")
```

Page 12 — Warm-Up
Q1 No — a quotation mark is missing after the first bracket.
Q2 Syntax error
Q3 Colour coding
Q4 A chatbot
Q5 Return (or Enter)

Page 12 — Practice Questions
Q1 It displays text on screen.
Q2 False
True
True — if you start with a single quotation mark you must end with a single quotation mark too (similarly for double quotation marks).
Q3 `input("What is your favourite colour? ")`
`print("Thank you, I won't remember that.")`
Q4 E.g.
- a question and answer program (or chatbot)
- a mathematical calculator program
- a contacts list program
- a drawing program

Q5
```
print("I'm going to ask some questions.")
input("What is your name?")
print("Cool name...")
input("Do you put pineapple on pizza?")
print("I'm the same!")
```

Answers

Page 13 — What is a Variable?
Q1 `surname` and `name1` are valid variable names.
'first name' is invalid as it contains a space.
'1stNAME' is invalid because it begins with a number.
'Surname?' and '#name' are invalid because they contain a symbol other than an underscore.

Page 14 — Using Variables
Q1 Errors in the program have been circled.

```
name = input("Who are you?")
print(hello, username)
```

First error: quotation marks are missing around "hello".
Second error: the user's input is stored in a variable called `name`, not `username`.

Page 15 — Warm-Up
Q1 Equals sign (=)
Q2 Variable names are not allowed to include spaces.
Q3 Different variables, as they are capitalised differently.
Q4 Comma (,)
It could also be a plus sign (+) as you'll learn on p.16.
Q5 It is the wrong way round — the variable name should come before the value.

Page 15 — Practice Questions
Q1 A name in a program used to store a value.
Q2 The missing words are:
  a) underscore
  b) Numbers
Q3 Upper camel case — SuperCar
Lower camel case — maxHeight
Snake case — battery_level
Q4 a)
```
4   shopTotal = apples + bread + milk
5   print(shopTotal)
```
  b) 10
  The value of the variable `shopTotal` is the sum of the values of the variables `apples`, `bread` and `milk`.
Q5 False
True
True

Page 16 — Controlling On-Screen Text
Q1 E.g.
`print("I <3\nPython")`

Page 17 — Warm-Up
Q1 Add/plus (+)
Q2 Backslash (\)

Page 17 — Practice Questions
Q1 Joining two strings together to create one longer string.
Q2 E.g.
```
If you mix yellow and blue you get? green
What year were you born? 40000BC
green40000BC
```

Q3 a) \n is used to add a new line when printing.
  b) Multiple lines of text can be printed with a single line of code.
Q4 Errors in the program have been circled.

```
print("Choose an even number between 1 and 10 but don't tell m(e)
(numbre) = input("Type in your number and I promise not to look: ")
print("I guess your number was (:)number")
```

First error: a quotation mark is missing.
Second error: the variable name 'number' is spelt incorrectly.
Third error: a colon is used instead of a comma.
Q5 E.g.
```
age = input("Enter age: ")
print("Cheers to " + age + " years.\nAnd many more!")
```
You could also have done this using commas instead of plus signs.

Page 18 — Coding Challenges
Head to cgpbooks.co.uk/ks3-python-extras to download an example program for each challenge.

Section Three — Data Types and Operators

Page 19 — Data Types
Q1 a) Float
  b) String
  c) Boolean
  d) Integer

Pages 20-21 — How to Handle Strings
Q1 The wrong variable has been printed (in the last line, `text` should be `upperText`).
Q2
```
word = "strawberry"
rCount = word.count("r")
print(rCount)
```
Q3 a
Q4 a

Page 22 — Warm-Up
Q1 To count the number of characters in a string.
Q2 count
Q3 0
Q4 The last character.

Page 22 — Practice Questions
Q1

Boolean	True or False
Integer	e.g. 10
String	"Think of a number"
Float	e.g. 12.5

Q2 a) Integer (or Float)
  b) Casting

Answers

Q3
```
totalDistance = 100
distanceRun = str(input("How far have you run? "))
remainingDistance = totalDistance - distanceRun
print("Distance left is ", remaining)
```
First error: the input should be cast to an integer using `int`.
Second error: the variable name is incorrect — it should be `remainingDistance`.

Q4 a) 9
b) 3

Q5
```
username = input("Enter username: ")
first = username[0]
last = username[-1]
print(first + "******" + last)
```
You need to use + to concatenate instead of commas in the print function, otherwise you'd get spaces between the parts.

Pages 23-24 — Working with Integers and Floats
Q1 The missing operator is: /
Q2 Each `int()` function should be replaced by a `float()` function.

Page 25 — Warm-Up
Q1 Float
Q2 All inputs are strings, so you need to cast to integers or floats before you can do arithmetic operations.
Q3 9.0
Remember, calculations involving floats will result in a float.

Page 25 — Practice Questions
Q1 Float
Q2 The multiplication symbol be * not ×.
The division symbol should be / not \.
Q3 a)
```
a = 60
b = 4
c = a / b
print(c)
15.0
```
b)
```
a = 20
b = 100 - a
print(b)
80
```
c)
```
a = 52
b = a + 48
print(b)
100
```

Q4 a) 2.0
b) 9.9
c) 0
d) 9

Page 26 — Relational Operators
Q1 E.g.

`a = "kettle"` `b = "teapot"` `print(a == b)`	`a = 10` `b = 10` `print(a != b)`	`a = 1` `print(a < 2)` `print(a > 2)`	`a = 60` `print(a <= 50)` `print(a >= 50)`
False	False	True False	False True

Page 27 — Boolean Operators
Q1 a)
```
a = False
b = True
c = a and b
print(c)
False
```
b)
```
a = False
b = False
c = a or b
print(c)
False
```
c)
```
a = True
b = not a
print(b)
False
```

Page 28 — Warm-Up
Q1 <=
Q2 and, or and not
Q3 and
Q4 not

Page 28 — Practice Questions
Q1 == — Equal to
>= — Greater than or equal to
!= — Not equal to
< — Less than
Q2 a) False
b) True
c) True
Q3 `licence = age >= drivingAge`
Q4 a) True
b) True
c) False

Page 29 — Coding Challenges
Head to cgpbooks.co.uk/ks3-python-extras to download an example program for each challenge.

Section Four — Selection
Some answers in this section show only part of a program. Python files containing the full code can be downloaded at cgpbooks.co.uk/ks3-python-extras.

Page 30 — Selection
Q1
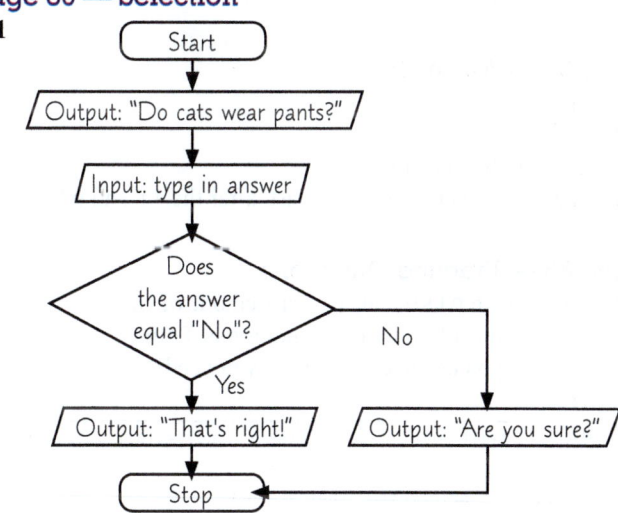

Page 32 — Warm-Up
Q1 Sequence, selection and iteration
Q2 Sequence
Q3 Diamond
Q4 == should be used instead of =

Answers

Page 32 — Practice Questions

Q1 E.g. a selection statement can be change the path of a program based on user input or variable values.

Q2
```
temp = int(input("Enter a temperature
if temp >= 0:
print("Correct, well done")
```

First error: this is a logic error — a user is only correct if they enter a temperature of 0 or below, so the operator `<=` should be used instead.

Second error: this is a syntax error — this line of code should be indented.

Q3 a) `% remaining: 15`
b) `Obviously not!`
   `Thanks for playing.`

Q4 E.g. two of the following:
- `if` must be written in lowercase
- there must be a colon at the end of the line
- the code inside the `if` statement must be indented
- the code after the `if` statement must be unindented

Q5 3 `number2 = input("Enter the larger number: ")`
4 `if number1 == "1" and number2 == "7":`

Page 33 — The else Clause

Q1 E.g. the following line should be added on the second line, following the user input:
`day = day.lower()`

Page 34 — The elif Clause

Q1 `Come on now, I said one to three stars.`
None of the conditions are true, so the else clause is used.

Page 35 — Warm-Up

Q1 `or`
Q2 `elif`
Q3 It should be indented.
Q4 The `else` clause should be last, after the `if` and `elif`s.

Page 35 — Practice Questions

Q1 False — the `else` clause is carried out when the `if` statement condition is `True`.
False — you can use as many as you need.
True

Q2 a)
```
1  digit = int(input("Enter a single-digit multiple
2  if digit == 4 or digit == 8:
3      print("Yep, that's right.")
4  else digit == 0 or digit == -4 or digit == -8:
5      print("You're a clever one ain't ya?")
6  else
7      print("That ain't right, sorry.")
```
First error: this should be an `elif` clause, not `else`.
Second error: a colon is missing at the end of the line.

b) Line 4:
`elif digit == 0 or digit == -4 or digit == -8:`
Line 5:
`else:`

Q3
```
1  score = int(input("Please enter your score: "))
2  if score >= 30:
3      print("Gold award — spectacular!")
4  elif score >= 20:
5      print("Silver award — brill!")
6  elif score >= 10:
7      print("Bronze award — well it's something!")
8  else:
9      print("Better luck next time...")
```

The condition `score >= 30` is used on line 2, as any score greater than or equal to 30 earns a gold award. If that condition is `false`, then you know the score is less than 30. This means you only need to check the lower boundary for the silver award, so the condition `score >= 20` can be used on line 4. Similarly, only the lower boundary for the bronze award needs to be checked on line 6, as by then you know the previous two conditions were both `false`.
You could also have used the conditions `score > 29`, `score > 19` and `score > 9` on lines 2, 4 and 6 respectively.

Page 36 — Coding Challenges

Head to cgpbooks.co.uk/ks3-python-extras to download an example program for each challenge.

Section Five — Iteration

Page 37 — Iteration

Q1 E.g.

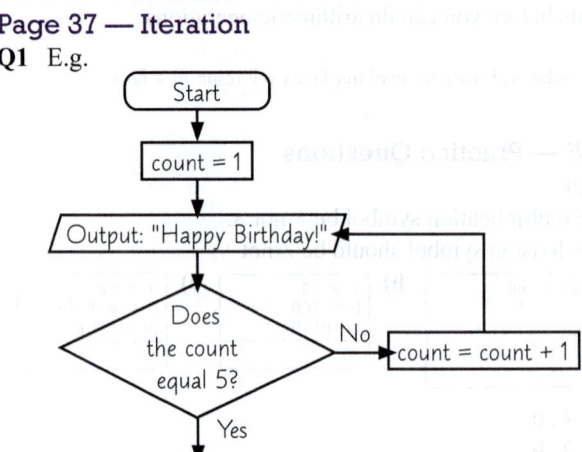

Page 38 — for Loops

Q1 `for i in range(3):`
      `print("Ho!")`

Q2 `myNumber`
The other options are not valid variable names — they cannot start with a number, or contain a space.

Page 39 — Warm-Up

Q1 There is a path that loops back to an earlier step.
Q2 True
Q3 A colon (`:`)

Answers

Page 39 — Practice Questions
Q1 Iteration is used to repeat code a number of times.

Q2 a)
```
for i in range(5):
    print("Is there anybody there?")
```
The circled line (print) should be indented.

b)
```
for i in range("ten"):
    print("Error")
```
A number should be used (10), not a string.

Q3 a) Get ready...
Get ready...
Get ready...
Go!

b) Hop forward
Step right
Hop forward
Step right

Q4
```
for i in range(3):
    print("For she's a jolly good fellow")
print("And so say all of us!")
```

Q5 E.g. one of the following:
- It reduces the amount of code you need to write, which saves time.
- It's easier to make changes to the code as you only have to make a change once, rather than multiple times in repeated code.

Pages 40-41 — Printing Numbers and Letters
Q1 The output would be:
0
1
Ride starting...

Q2 Square brackets have been used instead of round brackets.

Q3 7
8
9
10

Q4 a) 20 is the start value,
81 is the stop value,
30 is the step value.

b) 20
50
80

Q5
```
word = "Frog"
for letter in word:
    print(letter)
```

Page 42 — Warm-Up
Q1 False — it generates the sequence 0, 1, 2.
Q2 2, 3, 4
Q3 False — each letter should be on a new line.

Page 42 — Practice Questions
Q1 a) Control both the start and stop numbers of the sequence.
b) The step value.

Q2 a)
```
for i in range 10:
    print(i)
```
The stop value 10 should be in brackets.

b)
```
for i in range(0, 9, -1):
    print(i)
```
The values should be swapped — start value should be 9 and the stop value should be 0.
This one is a logic error — the syntax is perfectly fine!

Q3
```
word = "Guitar"
for i in range(len(word)):
    print(word[i])
```
You could have used a different name for the loop variable i.

Q4 range(11)
range(-5, 6)
range(101, 200)
range(100, 9, -1)
range(9, 2, -2)
The stop value here could also be 1.
range(9, 109, 9)
The stop value here could be any integer from 109 up to 117.

Page 43 — Coding Challenges
Head to cgpbooks.co.uk/ks3-python-extras to download an example program for each challenge.

Section Six — More Iteration

Pages 45-46 — while Loops
Q1 The input "guido van rossum" satisfies the `while` loop condition, as the `!=` operator is case sensitive, so the program will ask the user to try again.

Q2 For "crisps", the `category` condition is `False`, so the `while` loop never runs, regardless of the `price` entered.

Q3 `"what up"` and `"h+e+l+p"` are both rejected, as they're longer than 6 characters. `"12345"` and `"hey yo"` are accepted.
The program only checks the length of the input — not whether it's an actual word. Remember too, all characters are counted by `len()`, including spaces and symbols.

Page 47 — Nesting Statements
Q1 E.g. you could add an `else` clause to the first `if` statement.

Page 48 — Warm-Up
Q1 Condition-controlled
Q2 Click 'Interrupt Execution' in the Shell menu, or press the corresponding keyboard shortcut.
Q3 True

Answers

Page 48 — Practice Questions
Q1
```
cheer = "yes"
while cheer == "yes":
    print("Come on Raf!")
    cheer = input("Continue? ")
```
Q2
```
Enter a number: 10
5
Enter a number: 25
20
Enter a number: 35
Bye
```
Q3 a) First error: the loop condition is checking if the input is correct, but it should be checking the opposite.
Second error: `name` is not reassigned in the while loop, causing an infinite loop.

b) E.g.
```
name = input("Input a name: ")
while len(name) <= 3 or len(name) >= 15:
    print("Invalid name. Try again.")
    name = input("Input a name: ")
print("Success")
```
Q4 E.g. use a nested `if` statement:
```
word = input("Enter a word in lowercase: ")
for letter in word:
    if letter != letter.lower():
        print("Bad:", letter)
    else:
        print("Good:", letter)
```

Page 49 — Coding Challenges
Head to cgpbooks.co.uk/ks3-python-extras to download an example program for each challenge.

Section Seven — Lists

Page 50 — Lists
Q1 1 and −3

Page 51 — Working with Lists
Q1 `sports[2] = "Golf"`
You could have used the index −1 instead of 2.

Page 52 — Warm-Up
Q1 An organised collection of items stored under one name.
Q2 False.
The first item in a list has index 0.
Q3 Square brackets must be used to access items in a list, not round brackets. So the second line should be:
`print(numbers[2])`

Page 52 — Practice Questions
Q1 a) Strings
b) i) 6
  ii) hate
c) `print("I", words[0], "to put", words[4], "on my", words[2])`
This answer column couldn't handle such a marvellous bit of code — you'll have to imagine it as a single line.
d) The string `"crocodile"` does not exist in the list.
Q2 `.append()` adds an item to the end of a list, whereas `.insert()` places an item inside a list at a particular index.
Q3 `['Fish', 'Cat', 'Snake']`
`['Fish', 'Budgie', 'Snake']`
`['Fish', 'Budgie', 'Ferret', 'Rabbit']`

Page 53 — Iterating Through Lists
Q1 E.g.
```
integers = [1, 2, 3, 4, 5, 6]
for number in integers:
    print("Double", number, "is", number * 2)
```

Page 55 — Warm-Up
Q1 False
The index of the last item is one less than the length of a list.
Q2 In order of the item's indexes, starting from 0.
Q3 `myList[0][0]`

Page 55 — Practice Questions
Q1 a) E.g.
```
for i in range(len(noises)):
    if len(noises[i]) < 4:
        print(noises[i])
```
b) E.g.
```
for word in noises:
    if len(word) < 4:
        print(word)
```

Q2

Code	Output
`print(groups[0][1])`	AJ
`print(groups[0][0])`	Jess
`print(groups[1])`	`['Igor', 'Tobi', 'Eve']`
`print(groups[1][1])`	Tobi
`print(groups[2][1])`	Luiza

Q3 The program uses the values in the list as indexes, rather than printing the values itself.
The program prints three times, as the first three values in the list (4, 1 and 0) happen to be valid indexes. The fourth value (5) isn't a valid index, so causes the error.

Page 56 — Coding Challenges
Head to cgpbooks.co.uk/ks3-python-extras to download an example program for each challenge.

Answers

Section Eight — Subroutines

Pages 57-58 — Built-in Subroutines
Q1 a) E.g.
```
values = [5, 1, 4, 2, 3]
orderedValues = sorted(values)
print(orderedValues)
```
b) Ascending order (from lowest to highest).
c) `TypeError: '<' not supported between instances of 'int' and 'str'`
In sorting the list, the `sorted()` subroutine tried to compare a string with an integer using the relational operator <.

Page 59 — Warm-Up
Q1 A subroutine is a named block of code that performs a particular task.
Q2 `len()`
Q3 6
Q4 `import random`

Page 59 — Practice Questions
Q1 E.g.
- It's easier to use them than to write the code yourself.
- They're well-tested, so are unlikely to contain errors.

Q2 True
The list should be in square brackets: `sorted([1, 2, 3])`.
True
False

Q3 `[-6, -2, 1, 3, 5, 7, 15, 4]`

Q4 a)
```
words = ["turtle", "adverb", "magic", "nonsense", "flying"]
letter = input("Please enter a letter: ").lower()

total = 0
for i in range(len(words)):
    total = total + words[i].count(letter)

print("The letter was found", total, "times.")
```
b) The program counts the total number of times that the user's inputted letter appears in the words in the list.

Pages 60-61 — Defining Subroutines
Q1
```
def showMenu():
    print("Select an option (1-3).")
    print("1. Play 7 times table.")
    print("2. Play 9 times table.")
    print("3. Quit.")
```
Q2 E.g.
```
def play7TimesTable():
    for i in range(1, 13):
        print("Work out:", i, "x 7")
        answer = int(input("Answer: "))

        if answer == i * 7:
            print("Correct!")
        else:
            print("Wrong, it's", i * 7)

play7TimesTable()
```

Page 62 — Parameters
Q1 E.g.
```
welcomePlayer()
showMenu()
option = input("Option: ")

while option != "3":

    if option == "1":
        playTimesTable(7)
    elif option == "2":
        playTimesTable(9)
    else:
        print("Invalid option.")

    showMenu()
    option = input("Option: ")

print("Goodbye!")
```

Page 63 — Return Values
Q1 a) and b)
```
def welcomePlayer():
    name = input("Hi! What's your name? ")
    print("Welcome to the quiz", name)
    return name
```
```
name = welcomePlayer()
choice = getMenuChoice()

while choice != "3":

    if choice == "1":
        playTimesTable(7)
    elif choice == "2":
        playTimesTable(9)
    else:
        print("Invalid option.")

    choice = getMenuChoice()

print("Goodbye", name)
```
This is a modification of the program from Q1 on p.62. You could have also modified the first version from p.61.

Page 64 — Warm-Up
Q1 The indentation of the code ends.
Q2 False — function names cannot start with a number and cannot contain symbols, other than underscores.
Q3 `.insert()`
It takes two parameters — an index and an item.
Q4 One

Answers

Page 64 — Practice Questions
Q1 E.g. by breaking down complex programs into smaller subroutines.

Q2 a) Four — `range`, `input`, `len` and `print`.
   b) i) `repeat`
   ii) 1. `text`
         2. `n`
   iii) `result`
   c) `haha` and `hahahahahahahaha`

Q3 a)
```
def playTimesTable(n):
    score = 0
    for i in range(1, 13):
        print("Work out:", i, "x", n)
        answer = int(input("Answer: "))

        if answer == i * n:
            print("Correct!")
            score = score + 1

    return score
```

b) E.g.
```
result = playTimesTable(7)
print("You scored:", result)
```

Page 65 — Coding Challenges
Head to cgpbooks.co.uk/ks3-python-extras to download an example program for each challenge.

Section Nine — Turtle Graphics

Pages 67-68 — Simple Shapes
Q1 E.g.
```
from turtle import *

forward(300)
left(90)
forward(100)
left(90)
forward(300)
left(90)
forward(100)
```

Q2 E.g.
```
from turtle import *

forward(75)
right(90)
forward(200)
left(90)
forward(75)
right(90)
forward(75)
right(90)
forward(150)
right(90)
forward(275)
```

Q3 E.g.
```
from turtle import *

forward(100)
right(120)
forward(100)
right(120)
forward(100)
right(120)
```

Q4 E.g.
```
from turtle import *

right(90)
forward(300)
penup()
left(90)
foward(100)
left(90)
pendown()

forward(300)
hideturtle()
```

Page 69 — Warm-Up
Q1 a) Right
   b) Shown
   c) Down

Q2 Pixels

Q3 False — the turtle stays facing in the same direction.

Q4 `right(90)`

Page 69 — Practice Questions
Q1

Code	Description
`from turtle import *`	Loads all the subroutines from the `turtle` module.
`backward(150)`	Moves the turtle 150 pixels in the opposite direction to where its facing.
`left(20)`	Turns the turtle 20 degrees anticlockwise.

Answers

Q2 E.g.
```
from turtle import *

forward(100)
left(120)
forward(100)
left(120)
forward(100)

left(30)
forward(100)
left(90)
forward(100)
left(90)
forward(100)

hideturtle()
```

Q3

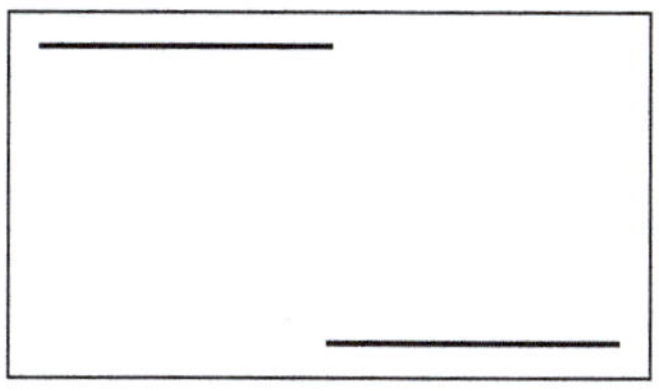

Page 70 — Polygons and Circles
Q1 E.g.
```
from turtle import *

for i in range(3):
    forward(100)
    left(120)

hideturtle()
```

Q2 E.g.
```
from turtle import *

def drawPolygon(n):
    for i in range(n):
        forward(100)
        left(360 / n)

sides = int(input("How many sides? "))
drawPolygon(sides)

hideturtle()
```
If the turtle starts drawing off the screen, you can lower the number in the `forward()` command to draw a smaller shape.

Q3 E.g.
```
from turtle import *

circle(50)
left(180)
circle(100)

hideturtle()
```

Page 71 — Adding Colours
Q1 E.g.
```
from turtle import *

fillcolor("Blue")
begin_fill()
forward(100)
left(120)
forward(100)
left(120)
forward(100)
left(120)
end_fill()

fillcolor("Red")
begin_fill()
forward(100)
right(120)
forward(100)
right(120)
forward(100)
right(120)
end_fill()

hideturtle()
```

Q2 E.g.
```
from turtle import *

pencolor("Orange")
for i in range(4):
    pensize(i * 5)
    forward(100)
    right(90)

hideturtle()
```

Page 72 — Stars and Random Shapes
Q1 E.g.
```
from turtle import *

def drawStar(numberOfPoints, sideLength):
    for i in range(numberOfPoints):
        forward(sideLength)
        left(360 / numberOfPoints)
        forward(sideLength)
        right(720 / numberOfPoints)

drawStar(6, 50)
hideturtle()
```
The original n parameter has also been renamed to `numberOfPoints` so that it's easier to understand what the two parameters are for.

Page 73 — Warm-Up
Q1 The radius of the circle (in pixels).
Q2 The spelling — it should be `bgcolor`.
Q3 `pensize()`
Q4 True

Answers

Page 73 — Practice Questions

Q1 a) E.g.
```
from turtle import *
bgcolor("Green")
circle(100)
right(90)
backward(200)
hideturtle()
```

b) E.g.
```
from turtle import *
pensize(10)
pencolor("Red")
for i in range(4):
    forward(20)
    penup()
    forward(20)
    pendown()
hideturtle()
```

Q2 E.g.
```
from turtle import *
import random

bgcolor("AliceBlue")
sides = random.randint(3, 15)

fillcolor("PapayaWhip")
begin_fill()

for i in range(sides):
    forward(100)
    right(360 / sides)

end_fill()

hideturtle()
```

Q3

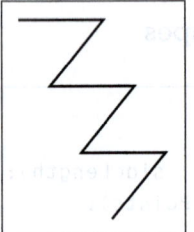

Page 74 — Coding Challenges

Head to cgpbooks.co.uk/ks3-python-extras to download an example program for each challenge.

Section Ten — Longer Challenges

Answers to this section are in Python files which can be downloaded from cgpbooks.co.uk/ks3-python-extras.

The answers provided there are example programs — don't worry if your program doesn't match this code exactly, there are loads of different ways you could do them.

If you're really stuck getting started with a challenge, you could take a look at the example program or experiment with it first before trying to make the whole program yourself.

The Python files also contain example programs for each of the 'Going Further' suggestions in this section.

Index

A
algorithms 8
and (boolean operator) 27, 31
.append() 51
arithmetic operators 23, 24
ASCII art 16
asterisk (import *) 66

B
backward() 66
begin_fill() 71
bgcolor() 71
blocks 30
boolean
    data type 19
    operators 27, 46
built-in subroutines 57, 58

C
calling 60
camel case 13
case sensitivity 19
casting 19, 24
characters
    escape characters 16
    string characters 20, 21
chatbot 11, 14, 34
circle() 70, 71
clauses
    elif clauses 34
    else clauses 33
color (turtle) 71
commas 14, 50, 62
concatenation 16
condition
    elif conditions 34
    if conditions 31
    while loop conditions 45, 46
condition-controlled loops 44-46
.count() 20
count-controlled loops 38-41, 44

conventions 13
cursor 66

D
data structures 50
data types 19
decomposition 60
defining (subroutines) 60-63
definite loops 38-41, 44
drawing (using turtle) 66-74

E
editor window (IDLE) 3, 5
elif 34
else 33
end_fill() 71
errors 6, 7, 10, 81
escape characters 16
exclusive 40

F
false (boolean value) 19, 26, 27
fillcolor() 71
float() 19, 24
floats (data type) 19, 23, 24
flowcharts 8
    of for loops 37
    of if statements 30
    of while loops 44
for loops 38-41
forward() 66

H
hello, world 7
hideturtle() 68

I
IDE (integrated development environment) 3
IDLE 3-5
    editor window 5
    shell window 4
if statements 31-34
import (modules) 58, 66
inclusive 40
indefinite loops 44-46
indentation 31
index position
    lists 50, 51
    strings 21
input() 11
input (in the Shell) 4
.insert() 51
installing Python 3
int() 19
integers (data type) 19, 23
iteration
    block type 30
    for loops 37-41
    this entry 93
    through lists 53
    while loops 45, 46

J
joke 47

L
left() 67
len() 20, 50
line numbers 7
lists 50-53
    2D lists 54
logic errors 6
loops 37, 44
    for loops 38-41
    while loops 45, 46
.lower() 20
lowerCamelCase 13

Index

M
modules 58
   random 58, 72
   turtle 66

N
naming conventions 13
nesting statements 47
new line (escape character) 16
not (boolean operator) 27

O
open source software 2
operators
   arithmetic 23, 24
   boolean 27, 46
   relational 26, 27
or (boolean operator) 27, 33
output (in the Shell) 4

P
parameters 62
pen (turtle) 66
   pencolor() 71
   pendown() 68
   pensize() 71
   penup() 68
pixel 66
polygon 70
print() 10
program
   decomposition 60
   making and running 5
   planning 8
pseudocode 8
Python 2-80

R
.randint() 58, 72
random (module) 58, 72
range() 38, 40, 41, 53
relational operators 26, 27
.remove() 51
return values 63
right() 67

S
selection 30
sequence 30
shell window (IDLE) 3, 4
showturtle() 68
.shuffle() 80
snake_case 13
sorted() 58
start value 40
step value 41
stop value 40
str() 19
string characters 20, 21
string handling 20, 21
strings (data type) 19
subroutines
   built-in 57, 58
   user-defined 60, 63
sum() 57
syntax errors 6

T
true (boolean value) 19, 26, 27
turtle graphics 66-72
two-dimensional lists 54

U
.upper() 20
UpperCamelCase 13
user-defined subroutines 60, 63
user input 11

V
variables 13, 14

W
while loops 45, 46

X
x (as an unimaginative variable name) 23, 24